AN INVITATION TO TRAVEL

HILARY EMBERTON

Library of Congress Registration Number
VAU001171827

ISBN 978-0-9861451-0-0

To My Husband Don

For steering me in the right direction and keeping me on a steady course.

Not all who wander are lost.
J.R.R. Tolkien

The most dangerous worldview is the worldview of those who have not viewed the world.
Alexander von Humboldt

PREFACE

In 1989, sitting at my office desk, a thought came into my head: "There's got to be more to life than this."
The thought stayed. My life was comfortable enough. Maybe that was the problem; I needed something more than
comfortable. By 1991 I had left the U.K. to travel the world, and never made it back. I still travel.
Along the way I have met countless kind people, seen amazing things and broadened my cultural horizon. Travel
opens your mind and your heart. The following photo-based essays are small glimpses of the world, but I hope they
provide some insight into the marvelous commotion that is our globe.

CONTENTS

Preface   4

BHUTAN: Domkhar, April 2013   9

RWANDA: Parc National des Volcans, February 2004   11

MONGOLIA: Lake Khovsgul, July 2008   13

PANAMA: Nalunega Island, San Blas Islands, March 1992   14

CZECH REPUBLIC: Prague, October 1999   17

NEW ZEALAND: Mitre Peak, Milford Sound, December 2000   19

MALTA: Valletta, September 2005   20

CUBA: Havana, January 1997   23

SOUTH KOREA: Seongsan, Jeju-Do, September 1991   25

TIBET: Rongbuk, Himalayas, September 2006   26

SRI LANKA: Anuradhapura, February 2003   29

CANADA: Blanley Bay, Nunavut, August 2011   31

LEBANON: Tripoli, March 2001   32

PERU: Ingenio, Central Highlands, September 2001   35

UGANDA: Kyabirwa, October 2007   37

VIETNAM: Sapa, April 1995   38

TUNISIA: Sidi Bou Said, September 2008   41

NAMIBIA: Sossusvlei, April 2004   43

RUSSIA: St. Petersburg, August 2008   45

THAILAND: Nan, February 1995   46

SINGAPORE: Kampong Glam Cemetery, November 2000   49

SPAIN: Palma, Mallorca, January 2008   51

TURKEY: Kapıkırı, July 2007   53

IRAN: Mashhad, September 2009   55

CHILE: Chiu Chiu, November 1997   56

KENYA: Maasai Mara National Park, February 2007   59

JORDAN: Jerash, March 1990   61

ICELAND: Reykjavik, June 2011   63

INDIA: Lake Nagin, Kashmir, August 1989   65

JAPAN: Miyajima Island, September 1991   66

ECUADOR: Galapagos Islands, April 1992   69

GUATEMALA: Antigua, November 1993   71

NEPAL: Chobhar, September 2006   73

ETHIOPIA: Kora Anbessa, January 2007   75

FRENCH POLYNESIA: Tahiti, June 1992   76

INDONESIA: Boti, Timor, May 2012   79

BOTSWANA: Chobe, April 2004   81

SYRIA: Job Mady, March 2001   83

COOK ISLANDS: Aitutaki, June 1992   84

CHINA: Chengdu, May 1999   87

UNITED KINGDOM: London, October 2005   89

CHILE: Rapa Nui (Easter Island), November 1997   90

MONGOLIA: Ulaanbaatar, July 2008   93

AUSTRALIA: Uluru-Kata Tjuta National Park, June 1994   95

LIBYA: Ghadames, October 2005   97

CAMBODIA: Tonlé Sap, June 1999   98

ANTARCTICA: Antarctic Peninsula, February 1997   101

MEXICO: Felipe Carrillo Puerto, December 1990   103

MALAYSIA: Mount Kinabalu, Borneo, February 2010   105

BELIZE: Punta Gorda, December 1994   107

MYANMAR: Le-in-go, January 1995   108

SOUTH AFRICA: Storms River Mouth, October 1996   111

TAIWAN: Fokuangshan, November 1991   113

MADAGASCAR: Kirindy National Park, October 2004   115

LAOS: Muang Ngoi, February 1995   116

HONG KONG: Hong Kong Island, December 1991   119

INDIA: Chandigarh, December 2010   121

CANADA: Montreal, September 1998   123

UNITED STATES: Nevada City, September 2010   125

THE AUTHOR: Ayacucho, Peru, September 2001   127

Acknowledgements   128

BHUTAN

At a religious festival at Domkhar, beautifully embroidered scarves were draped over the left shoulders of the women who, linked by their little fingers, swayed together and sang a song of Bhutan. A dancer representing a hero victorious over evil spirits was dressed in a bunched yellow skirt, elaborate bodice, and a crown. He turned in swirls with graceful elegance, swooping to the ground and arching to the sky to achieve equilibrium between man and universe.

The Bhutanese, who are courteous and quick to smile, are fond of many other characters, including the Four Friends — an elephant, a monkey, a rabbit, and a bird — who work together in harmony and cooperation to achieve a common goal. The government has taken this concept further by implementing policies designed to promote economic progress in accord with the spiritual and emotional well-being of the people. These goals are supremely admirable, but perhaps not surprising from a country where the chief aim is not Gross National Product but Gross National Happiness.

In another temple, I was drawn to an old black and white photograph of a woman in fine silk robes and necklaces of large beads, whose mysterious face was softened by a faint smile. Her kind eyes held my gaze and drew me in: I stood absorbed by her, finding it hard to leave. In this sacred sanctuary I could not record her image, and departed carrying her as an already fading memory. Days later wandering amongst the bric-a-brac of a souvenir shop I reached out and touched a dark pink, tattered silk scarf embroidered in cheerful colors. I was told the scarf was old and sold by the man who had woven it, after being released from enslavement by the King. This abolition of slavery was a compassionate act encouraged by the King's mother. On asking further about this lady, I was led to a black and white photo on the wall from which the lady with the mysterious face looked at me once more. I could not help but buy the scarf.

April 2013

DOMKHAR
A costumed Buddhist dancer at a religious festival.

RWANDA

The infant climbed onto a log and stood unsteadily. It thumped its chest, promptly falling backwards into the soft undergrowth. After only twenty minutes of hiking along a path, and a few more minutes bushwhacking, our guide had led us to the gorilla group. My first glimpse was just a small, dark shape behind a bush, but it was a thrilling moment.

Suddenly, the group's enormous silverback crashed out of the vegetation and stood at full height beating his chest. The two people standing next to me fled, leaving me alone and insignificant in the shadow of this immense mass of fur and muscle. Having asserted his dominance, he sat down quietly to eat leaves, his arm gently around a juvenile scaling his fat tummy.

I continued, to find Akareruro, a playful young male. He appeared, walked to within an arm's length of me, and sat down. We gazed at each other transfixed until the guide moved me away. Akareruro lay on his back, arms and legs in the air and then, rolling on his side, rested his head on his arm with a dreamy gaze. Getting up, he climbed a small tree, and with immense strength effortlessly bent the trunk over until it snapped. He turned to look at me, then sat and munched on the leaves. Eventually the guide moved me on, but Akareruro quickly rose to follow, and coming to me, took hold of my forearm. I stood still, eyes averted, thinking for an instant he would pull me toward him, but after a few seconds he let go. I will never forget the softness of his hand and the gentleness of his grip.

February 2007

PARC NATIONAL DES VOLCANS
Akareruro rests his head on his arms in a dreamy gaze.

MONGOLIA

The grassland stretched to the horizon in a vast expanse. Herds of spirited horses roamed freely, galloping wildly. Nomads thundered past on their mounts, moving as one, each small but sturdy. Mongolians learn to ride before they can walk.

Our Russian-made vans arrived at a clutch of circular nomad tents, picked at random; no appointment was necessary. Hospitality is second nature to these people and, without hesitation, they held down the dog, invited us in, and served fermented mare's milk. Slices of dry bread were offered, with small gray lumps of tooth-breaking cheese. Later, as a special honor, the vodka appeared. The comfortable interior was furnished with brightly painted furniture, posters and a small Buddhist shrine.

In northern Mongolia, the Dukha people herd caribou. Their tepees, or *ortzes*, have spartan interiors, caribou-skin mats and bright blue flags adorning their animist shrines. I visited a family on the shores of Lake Khovsgul. They had come to sell carvings of caribou bone, supplementing their subsistence. Enkhtuya, the matriarch, invited me to sit. She was stirring flour, butter, and sugar in a pot over the fire; it was her specialty. She had a striking face, and was calm and wise. Although my guide interpreted, she made eye contact with me while she spoke. We talked about children, food, and life. We connected. Enkhtuya related the difficulty with disease and inbreeding of their dwindling caribou herds. She presented me with a bowl of the dessert: it tasted of cookie dough. Sitting on the simple bed, she lit a long thin cigarette. She inquired if I planned to return to Mongolia next year. I replied that I didn't know. "If you do," Enkhtuya proposed, "stay with me and we can spend some time together and chat." This woman, who was willing to cross cultural borders and be open to new ideas, had invited me to share her home. I was moved.

July 2008

LAKE KHOVSGUL
Enkhtuya makes dessert in her tepee.

PANAMA

Swinging my legs out of bed, I planted my feet on soft, cool sand. At Hotel San Blas, rooms were thatched bamboo huts on the beach. There was a crab hole under my bed. Toilets were located in a wooden shack at the end of the boat jetty and the place to wash was a little shed with a basin of water and a half-gourd scoop. The water, drawn from a shallow well at the center of the island, was slightly brackish.

The San Blas Islands, northeast of Panama, are home to the Kuna Indians, an indigenous group who feel more connected to their trading neighbors in Colombia than to Panamanians. In this matriarchal culture, women wear their wealth in the form of heavy gold nose rings, making their noses fashionably long. They dress in wonderfully vibrant clothes: bright orange and yellow headscarves, multicolored sarongs, and wide bands of beadwork on their arms and legs. Their blouses comprise puffed sleeves and bodice backs, with fronts called *molas*, made of hand-stitched layers of appliqué fabric in striking designs, from animals to geometric motifs. These artful conceptions originate from body-painting in the time when they wore no clothes. When they tire of the *mola*, the women remove the appliqué from the blouse and sew in a new one, selling the old to a passing tourist. Astute businesswomen, it was against their principles to be photographed unless I paid a quarter. As persistent sales-people, they seemed slightly impatient with persons like myself who are not born to shop.

My visit was only for the weekend, but I loved the island so much I decided to stay a few more days. It was just as well; three young Colombian men staying at the hotel hijacked the plane I was due to take the next morning.

March 1992

NALUNEGA ISLAND, SAN BLAS ISLANDS
An appliqué fabric design adorns the blouse of a Kuna woman.

CZECH REPUBLIC

Wandering down a cobbled lane in this fairy-tale city, I heard strains of Bach floating in the air. A soprano was singing an aria with such a mellifluous tone that I had to find her. The source was a record shop where the clerk with a quiet smile was doing a brisk trade in the CD. I soon found that the city breathed music and commended myself on finding a concert on my first night. It transpired that there was a profusion of musical choices every night of my visit. Great fun also was the rendition of Don Giovanni at the puppet theatre, conducted by a drunken Mozart and whose Donna Elvira had a temper tantrum worthy of any operatic diva.

Swimming upstream through a flotilla of Dutch nuns on the Charles Bridge I perused the thirty statues on its flanks. The marvelous Astronomical Clock on the Old Town Hall was a complex arrangement of gilded arcs, circles, and an eccentric dial depicting signs of the Zodiac. On the hour, the Apostles made guest appearances through two portals. Buildings sported murals and mosaics including the artsy graffiti of the John Lennon Wall. Green copper domes glinting with gold trim punctuated the skyline. Screens and windows of stained glass in the Art Nouveau style glowed with color. Often stone was carved into dynamic human forms, or simpler — a bell, half emerging from a building corner.

Situated on a hill, the vast Prague Castle dominated the capital with its numerous buildings and dark St. Vitus Cathedral. From the latter leaped a pantheon of hideous gargoyles, snouts dripping in the rain. On Golden Lane, where Franz Kafka once lived, sat an eerie bronze sculpture of a man on all fours, his back bowed by the weight of a giant skull, said to be inspired by one of Kafka's characters. Indeed, there were Kafkaesque references in many places, such as Hradčany Square, where a traffic mirror distorted the surrounding buildings, reminiscent of the bad dream that is a Kafka novel.

October 1999

HRADČANY SQUARE, PRAGUE
The distortion of buildings in a traffic mirror.

NEW ZEALAND

After purchasing a battered Nissan, I bumped around New Zealand for three months. With a favorable exchange rate, I could afford to be uncharacteristically daredevil. I jumped off a bridge into Kawarau Gorge with an elastic band tied to my feet. Harnessed to a young man in a paraglider, I hurtled off a lofty hill and, spiraling upward on a thermal, glided like a bird high across beautiful Lake Wakatipu. Swerving inches from sheer rocks on the Shotover River, seven startled people and I took the ride of a lifetime in a jet boat. At 5000 feet over Wanaka, my instructor and I, in tandem, gleefully threw ourselves from an airplane; just as the earth appeared to be approaching very fast, our parachute opened and we floated down, landing so perfectly that I simply stood up. When I wanted to taste travel of the old-fashioned kind, a young lady pilot flew me, complete with goggles, in a Tiger Moth. I experienced a thrilling landing in a helicopter on the fresh and gleaming Fox Glacier.

Delighting very much in the friendly, humorous, down-to-earth New Zealanders, I enjoyed their somewhat quirky installations. The public toilets at Kawakawa were decorated with colorful, oddly shaped glass and tiles. Glass bottles formed walls, and bulbous multi-colored pillars stood on mosaic floors. Of a more mechanical nature, Waiau Waterworks displayed water-powered gadgets and machines in all sorts of eccentric applications. The most whimsical was a man made of iron rods called "Bones" who pedals twenty-four miles a day on a stationary bicycle on the surface of a pond.

The glorious landscape of Milford Sound was a stunning location on the west coast of the South Island. Taking a boat trip, I rued the miserable rainy weather; the area is one of the wettest in the world. Soon understanding that it defined the beauty of the place, I opened my eyes and marveled at the ethereal quality of the mist. Dark, brooding hills receded in waning shades of gray, disappearing completely into the white formless infinity. It made me realize that often it is better to appreciate how things are, and not how we want them to be.

December 2000

MITRE PEAK, MILFORD SOUND
Dark, brooding hills recede in waning shades of gray.

MALTA

The entire city of Valletta is designated a UNESCO World Heritage Site, as "one of the most concentrated historic areas in the world." It was pure joy to walk the streets and marvel at its history. Compressed into a small space were buildings from the sixteenth, seventeenth, and eighteenth centuries, all in a warm beige limestone. The magnificent St. John's Cathedral, an excellent example of Maltese Baroque, contained two paintings by the master Caravaggio that were so beautiful I was moved to tears. Castles with towering bastions protected elegant edifices on narrow streets. Fine residences were decorated with detailed carving, lamps and letterboxes, and a wonderful selection of elaborate brass doorknockers. Casement windows in brown or muted green were cantilevered from upper floors. They were all deserted, but in my search for a perfect balcony, I saw an older woman staring vacantly, standing motionless as I took a picture. I thought she hadn't noticed me until a girl joined her and gave me a charming smile.

Attempts to speak the local language can require determination: I tried my best to speak Maltese. At Ġgantija, a 5000-year-old temple, the ticket clerk taught me *insalemlak* meaning hello. I tried it on the custodian at St. John's Cathedral, who frowned. When I explained that I was trying say hello in Maltese, his colleague informed me that they simply say hello. I asked for the word in their language and they scratched their heads and came up with *kivinti*. At the Knights Hospitallers Museum, I offered my best *kivinti*. They didn't understand until they realized I was trying to say *kifiniti*. Someone suggested that I could always use *caio*. But I didn't give up, and when a kind woman directed me to the Number Two bus I said *grazzi hafna* in thanks. She looked at me and gave my arm a little pat.

September 2005

VALLETTA
A woman and girl framed in a casement window.

CUBA

In Havana, I rented a tiny and somewhat grubby apartment for ten dollars a day. The water supply was intermittent and I enjoyed the company of a resident mouse in the kitchen. It was the perfect base to explore Havana and I started wandering the streets. Soon, I began to love the city. To fend off hustlers I developed a quick walk and preoccupied look. When I walked with a limp, the number of approaches decreased to zero. Cubans are compassionate after all.

The buildings in the city were an interesting mélange, from the ornate grandiose to the crumbling (whose sagging walls were often shored by timbers angled into the streets). In the empty spaces behind derelict facades, piles of rubbish were picked over by residents looking for food or useful items. I dined at eateries of two to three tables in the front rooms of private homes. The food was tasty and cheap. When buying rationed bread rolls for fifteen cents each, I paid for three, and was given four.

Music runs deep in the soul of every Cuban. Roaming the city, I heard melodies from all directions: bars, cafés, private houses, and from the many street musicians who sported large cigars and played their Latin music with consummate ease. At an open-mike venue, a couple sang a Cuban duet in beautiful harmony. I met them, discovering that surprisingly he was a neurosurgeon and she a pediatrician. Wandering to a crossroads, I heard a full-scale Salsa band practicing on an upper floor; I couldn't tell where, as the music bounced off the buildings at all four corners of the intersection. I stood for a while, totally enveloped in the quadraphonic sound. A man swept the road with a smile on his face, doing a little two-step shuffle to the music as he worked.

January 1997

HAVANA
Street musicians play their Latin music.

SOUTH KOREA

I started to fall in love with South Korea on the island of Jeju, not only because of the scenery, as that was certainly enchanting, but because Koreans were so friendly and such good fun. On the ferry to the island I was shepherded by two lady missionaries, the younger being the most joyful person I have ever met. Standing on deck, I savored the magical coastline of black volcanic rock and beautiful forested islands dotting the hazy horizon. Boisterous schoolboys, considering me a celebrity, talked to me in stammering and bashful English. I posed with them for photos in numerous and complex permutations.

The Manjang lava tube caves on Jeju were a spectacular remnant of an eruption. The eight-mile tube twisting and turning its way through the rock was twenty-five feet wide with an arched roof and flat floor like a vast subway tunnel. People continually greeted me as I walked through. On the return an amiable young man from a group of youths said something in Korean. I didn't understand, so he simply took my hand and we walked together, much to the amusement of his friends. His grasp was firm and confident as he softly sang Korean songs.

The bus to Seongsan or Sunrise Peak, a dramatic volcano jutting out to sea, passed a sedate procession of taxis transporting newlyweds on honeymoon. These couples played silly games on the grassy slopes of the crater. The girls wore *hanbok*, the national dress with voluminous sleeves, empire lines, and fluttering soft overskirts in shocking pink, red, or orange. In a hilarious relay race the grooms carried the girls around a course, either in their arms or piggyback. Comical as the latter may appear, it has a deeper and more serious significance, symbolizing the husband's acknowledgement of his responsibility to his new wife.

September 1991

SEONGSAN, JEJU ISLAND
Grooms carry their brides in a honeymoon game.

TIBET

Waking frequently in the night gasping for breath, I experienced terror and utter despair. In a tent on the Roof of the World at 16,400 feet, I had succumbed to altitude sickness. Abandoning sleep, I sat up for the rest of the night. At dawn, comfort arrived as guides dispensed cups of steaming tea, with a most gentle Tibetan "good mooorning." Emerging from a snow-dusted tent, I glanced in the direction of Everest through rain and hail and saw only a brooding fog.

The camp was at the Rongbuk Monastery, the loftiest in the world. Razed during the Cultural Revolution, it was being painstakingly rebuilt by monks and nuns. In this holiest of building sites, diminutive nuns wearing rubber boots were mixing concrete, while soft chanting wafted from above. Beautiful religious paintings decorated the walls of the simple temple. A nun turned a giant prayer wheel that rang a sonorous bell on each rotation.

A cart, drawn by a pony decorated with flags, tassels, and bells, transported me along the bumpy track to Everest Base Camp. The driver was kind and thoughtful and sang lilting soulful songs. The braid of hair wound round his head was tied with a red woolen scarf. The route was dramatic. Swirling mists fleetingly revealed craggy hills sprinkled with snow. Ahead in the rain a distant figure stood on a ridge; and beyond, the mountain was now just visible through a mass of stormy clouds. There was hope.

By the time the pony and cart trotted into base camp, the weather was clearing and I could feel the sun's warmth on my face. But one tenacious cloud still obscured the peak. Despite the off-season quiet, the white tents lining the main path offered tea and trinkets, or beds at Hotel California and Hotel Nescafé. Climbing a small hill adorned with prayer flags, I felt my heart leap. The last wisp of cloud had floated away, revealing Everest — crisp, clear and magnificent. How fortunate I was to be looking at the tallest mountain on Earth.

September 2006

RONGBUK, HIMALAYAS
Mt. Everest just visible through a mass of storm clouds.

SRI LANKA

Each morning before departing, Hary passed his hands around the steering wheel and then, joining them in prayer, invoked another safe day on the road. I had never hired a car and driver before, but Hary was trustworthy and careful, and called me "madam" the whole time. I encouraged Hary to drive to places he hadn't visited in a long while. I had to negotiate. "It is too dangerous, Madam," he said, "Tamils are there." "It will be fine, Hary, the troubles have ceased." We went, he found old friends; he had a good time.

Our trip was great fun. Sri Lanka was like India without the hassles. We happened upon a TV production for their Independence Day, with dancers, singers, and musicians. Among those waiting to perform stood tall, dark, beautiful girls elegantly dressed in blushing pink gowns.

I couldn't persuade Hary to go north. Deeply mistrustful of the Tamils, he put his foot down — on the brake. I decided to travel alone and met delightful people in a devastated war-torn region. I wandered past pockmarked shells of buildings, craters in streets, and government soldiers peering nervously from pillboxes shored up with sandbags, their guns trained on wary pedestrians. Periodically trucks full of soldiers roared by. The Norwegian-brokered peace was just a lull, everyone said, while the two sides regrouped. They were right. Not long after I left, the fighting resumed.

Two years later, Hary's daughter wrote that on a family outing to the beach Hary had died of a heart attack.

> "He was very happy that day. He came into the sea to bathe with us and for some time he was freely floating on the water happily with a smile on his face. Finally he gave his hand to me, then his eyes filled with tears and he withered like a flower on my hands."

The passing of a good soul.

February 2003

ANURADHAPURA
Girls in elegant gowns wait to perform.

CANADA

In Iceland, I boarded a ship that was en route from the Mediterranean to Thailand. In so doing, I became one of the privileged few who have traversed the Northwest Passage of the Canadian High Arctic. Once an unattainable goal, it is now possible due to the effects of a warming planet and eased by satellite imagery showing the location and density of the ice.

Exploring the small hamlets of the region, I was welcomed by Inuit with spontaneous smiles and curious dispositions. Our guide, whose modest demeanor belied a quiet confidence and a wealth of knowledge, exemplified the nature of these people. Marveling at his ability to spot animals, I saw a speck on the horizon transformed into a polar bear or a caribou or an Arctic hare. Cruising Blanley Bay in a small boat, he drew our attention to a herd of walrus cavorting in the water on a shoal. One massive walrus stayed resolutely grounded with its back to us, as if beached by its sheer bulk. After our third pass-by, possibly a little too close for comfort, the monstrous beast suddenly appeared by the boat, his tusks dangerously near the inflatable pontoons. Not fearful in the slightest, he fixed us with his bloodshot eyes for longer than we deemed to be idle curiosity. Many of us later admitted our hearts were in our mouths as we stared back at him, no more than a few feet away. Eventually his enormous body sank from view; no doubt satisfied he had sufficiently intimidated us.

Although the journey was relatively free of perils, the ship was only the 146th vessel to make the entire transit of the Northwest Passage from the Atlantic to the Pacific. I felt a gratifying sense of achievement on its completion.

August 2011

BLANLEY BAY, NUNAVUT
An intimidating walrus gives us the eye.

LEBANON

In the late 1960s my father visited Beirut on business. He spoke fondly of the culture and the fine architecture of "the Paris of the Middle East." More than thirty years later my sister and I witnessed a devastated city slowly and painfully rebuilding itself. The culture, however, still retained a European feel exemplified by girls without headscarves and wearing miniskirts.

The more orthodox northern city of Tripoli was an uproar of new unplanned development; but the old town citadel afforded a grand view of the maze of traditional markets, inns, bathhouses, mosques and schools below. A salvo of firecrackers heralded music with drums and cymbals. We hurried down to investigate and, following the sounds through narrow, crowded alleys, arrived at the hub of the celebration.

A beaming older couple dressed in white had returned from the *Hajj*, a pilgrimage to Mecca, culminating in a humdinger of a party. I was beckoned into a teeming courtyard to see two goats sacrificed, the ultimate accolade for the returnees. I thought I had lost my sister as a lady led me upstairs into a living room, where I became guest of honor as the pilgrims arrived. The room was embellished with tinsel streamers, and trays of candies and juice were served. As each guest entered the room they were embraced by the *hajjis*, and welcomed to the joyful gathering. Miraculously my sister arrived and a French-speaking chemistry teacher took us under her wing. Searching in my bag for a gift, I found a postcard of London's Tower Bridge. Requesting the chemistry teacher to write on it "Congratulations" in Arabic, I presented it to the pilgrims. It was respectfully accepted and courteously placed on a coffee table next to the plastic roses.

A simple postcard of a bridge was all I had to give, but the grace with which it was received reminded me that our presence was more important than any gift.

March 2001

TRIPOLI

Celebrating her arrival home, a hajji *embraces one of her guests.*

PERU

Juana, followed by the cat, brought in coca tea at the Peru Andino Guest House in Huancayo, high in the Andes. The tea was bitter but refreshing; the seemingly innocent leaves were an excellent remedy for my altitude headache and exhaustion from a grueling bus ride. On departing, Juana one-handedly picked up the cat by its two front legs. It didn't seem to mind.

The next day the gray cloud was so low I felt I could have bumped my head on it. Despite the oppressive weather, Juana's husband Luis was cheerful as we folded ourselves into a tiny bus. At times, the bus was so full there was barely room to breathe. A small boy boarded and recited the speech he'd said a hundred times before. I caught "*triste*" and "*noche*," from which I surmised he was sad in the night. He pulled out a crumpled bag of bonbons, describing the flavors in detail, before embarking to make his sales. Replacing him, a man sold booklets on diabetes. The irony was not lost on me. On exiting the bus, we squeezed through where no squeezing room could be seen.

Here in Ingenio, traditional Peruvian mountain music floated down from a nearby hill. An extended family was enjoying a fiesta. We were welcomed and offered *chicha*, the maize beer of the Andes. I steered clear of the more potent homemade hooch. The group was well-oiled and happy. They danced a minimalist shuffle. I gave it a try. The band was composed of a violinist, a man playing a spiral animal horn or *cornetta de cacho*, and a lady with a *tinga*, a small tambourine. She sang high-pitched notes that drifted though the air with an unearthly and haunting quality.

In the following days, my epic bus rides continued along the Central Highlands. The condition of the buses deteriorated until eventually I boarded a bus with a "For Sale" sign on the front. Luckily they didn't sell it during the journey.

March 2001

INGENIO, CENTRAL HIGHLANDS
A musician plays the cornetta de cacho.

UGANDA

The welcome in Uganda was enthusiastic. Children and adults alike smiled and waved, as if everyone in the country was the official greeter. By the end, my hand that waved was a little tired. The hilly terrain to Kyabirwa village was almost entirely cultivated; a bent back in every field.

A young man, Posiano Emoot, gave a tour of the village. He was well-dressed, courteous, and spoke excellent English. His grandmother's garden was a jumbled jungle of plants, but Posiano verbally untangled them, describing the use of each and every one. All garden plots are worked cooperatively by the extended family, and fenced using the vegetation itself. Sticks woven into a distinctive beehive shape, sealed inside with mud and dung, and topped with a thatched hat formed a storage place for millet and maize. Grandma's kitchen was in a spartan stick-and-mud hut with no more than a fire pit, a few pans and a grindstone. Posiano's own family home was also simple. In a small, tidy bedroom wallpapered with newsprint, his clothes hung on a line over his bed, and textbooks — including a Turkish phrase book — rested on a battered blue tin trunk. An oil lamp perched on a table by his bed, for there was no electricity. Indeed, water had to be fetched from a pump in the village and clothes washed in the river, half a mile distant.

The house to remember was painted in two earth colors, umber and ochre, accented with tangerine flowers and white triangles, proclaiming the words "A HOUSE TO ADMIRE." The owner worked in her yard drying maize, cassava and sorghum, with chickens in attendance. It confirmed my belief that regardless of your circumstances, it makes a world of difference to be proud of and appreciative for what you have.

October 2007

KYABIRWA

A house to admire.

VIETNAM

Newly arrived, I sat in a Hanoi café wondering what to do next. In walked Charlie, an Australian whom I had met in Laos. "I'm going to rent a motorbike," he announced. "Do you want to come?" Charlie rode the bike like a cowboy taming a wild stallion. However, it was at low speed on the appalling roads that we fell over eight times. Each time I daintily stepped away, pulling the machine off an increasingly battered and bruised driver.

We had a wonderful time exploring northern Vietnam. When we arrived at a village not previously visited by tourists, the officials were perplexed. At a Communist Party Committee meeting they decided we should return to Hanoi the next day. We honestly tried, but taking wrong turns on roads resembling mountain-bike trails, we ended up nearer the Chinese border. In another village, in lieu of a hotel, we chose to stay with a charming couple who welcomed us into their home.

My perch on the bike afforded a 300-degree view of stunning scenery. White thatched houses were nestled in vivid green rice fields dotted with limestone pinnacles. We drove across one of the many narrow wire-and-bamboo suspension bridges that in a graceful bow span thickly wooded ravines and river canyons. Heading toward Sapa, the landscape became intensely cultivated. Every foot of hillside had been terraced with rice fields of lime green, dark cool green or muted gold. This was the home of the friendly Hmong people who effortlessly stride these slopes. They are strikingly dressed in cloth of deep indigo with lighter blue or red trim. The women wear their long hair swirled on their heads capped by small pillbox hats, and adorn themselves with large silver hoop earrings, chains and bracelets. On market days they come to town with capacious woven baskets on their backs.

Back in Hanoi when the trip was over and Charlie had departed, I sat in a café, wondering what to do next. In walked Paul, whom I had met in Sapa. "I'm going to buy a motorbike and go south," he announced. "Do you want to come?"

April 1995

SAPA
Hmong girls look out over rice fields.

TUNISIA

Vowing never to visit another Islamic country during Ramadan, the month of fasting, I found myself with my husband in Tunisia — during Ramadan. With no eating, drinking or smoking permitted in daylight hours, people take life quietly and sleep a lot. The towns were deserted, dust blew in circles, doors and windows were firmly shuttered. Cafés and restaurants were closed. I wasn't seeing life in Tunisia. We were allowed to eat discreetly on a restaurant terrace hidden from public view, and sampled delicious seafood. I struggled with French till the waiter said, "Why don't we speak English? It's much easier."

An exception to the Ramadan hiatus was found in the touristy, but delightful, village of Sidi Bou Said near Carthage. Whitewashed houses all had doors and windows in a charming blue, framed with tumbling bougainvillea. Elegant archways over narrow cobbled lanes enticed us to explore. Exquisite tiled courtyards were filled with plants or fountains or birdcages or waiting glasses of tea. Open stairs led to rooftop patios and comfortable divans to admire a view.

Friendly merchants did a bustling trade with cruise ship inmates on shore leave. We bargained for a beautiful large shallow bowl, hand-painted with an intricate peacock-tail design. My husband dropped his camera, breaking a few dishes. The young vendor assured us with a genuine smile that it didn't matter. We gave him ten dinars as compensation. He gave us more bowls.

We lingered until dusk when suddenly — regardless of potential sales — all the retailers in town closed their shops. It was time for them to eat, drink and smoke. As the rest of Tunisia came to life, this corner of Tunisia became deserted.

September 2008

SIDI BOU SAID
Bougainvillea frames a door and window.

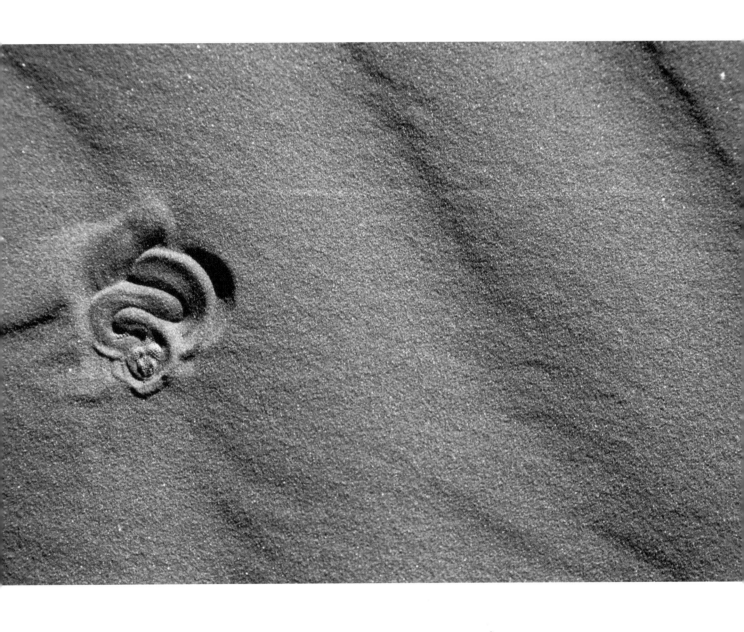

NAMIBIA

The crisp line dividing ebony and chestnut curved elegantly down the dune from apex to base, in a manner only a gifted artist could accomplish. When the air was still, there was utter silence. When the wind blew, sand whipped off the edge in spirals, to land again in a relentless forward march. At the summit, a wondrous sight of graceful crescents spread as far as the eye could see; crests rising and falling in an ocean of sand. The daily range of light played out a dynamic and colorful palette of reds, browns and blacks, chocolate, cinnamon, burnt peach, beige at dawn and vermilion at sunset. Textures varied as dense ripples flowed into smooth sand flowing into lines, furrows, and ridges. The impetus of a footstep sent an avalanche down the slopes in glinting veils or threw up a spray of fine particles much lighter and brighter than those underfoot.

In a cirque of sand hills, a group of wizened dead trees stood victim to a change in river course, black ghosts on a white salt lake. But the dunes were a hive of activity. A red and black beetle, making a burrow, pushed out small heaps with its back legs, then with sturdy front legs fanned them into mounds making a scallop shape. Bird tracks meandered in and out, punctuated by small holes. A black beetle scuttled using the natural lines of contour as footpaths. The swishing of grasses in the wind produced arced scratches on the sand. The tracks of a small lizard changed mysteriously into a continuous groove along a slope, sometimes crossing itself, only to inexplicably change to tracks again. A sidewinding snake lurked in the sand waiting for prey, its imprint an exquisite hieroglyph.

This was indeed an extraordinary outdoor gallery of nature's art.

April 2004

SOSSUSVLEI
The exquisite hieroglyph made by a sidewinding snake.

RUSSIA

It can take a journey of some 3000 miles, from the border of Mongolia to St. Petersburg, to realize the vastness of Russia. Traveling the Trans-Siberian Railway was a excellent way to admire the beauty of endless birch forests dotted with *dachas*, little wooden cottages fringed by substantial gardens spilling into the land beyond. The further west I went, the less Asian and the more European the feel. Nearly every little town had a large and splendid white station, with a green or pink trim. Many interiors were decorated with murals.

The trains were reassuringly punctual, but confusingly ran on Moscow time. They ranged from the basic — bunking with ladies and gentlemen alike — to the more luxurious, with satin bedspreads and a special tea set. The uniformed *provodnitsa* (conductress) who supervised each car could be formidable and kindly at the same time. One of her most important roles was making sure the samovar was topped up for continuous hot water. Asking my *provodnitsa* if I could purchase the Ural Railway teapot in my compartment, I was met with a resounding *nyet*, but it didn't take long for her to soften and realize the potential of a business deal.

At the journey's end in St. Petersburg, I lost my way in unfamiliar terrain and the strange alphabet, and asked a newspaper lady for directions. Like so many Russians, her gruff demeanor belied a heart of gold; she laid her papers down and personally escorted me to the correct bus, making sure the driver knew my intended destination. It was a surreal experience arriving at Peterhof Palace, where sumptuous gardens were adorned with ornate gold statuary and the fine white sparkling strands of the fountains. The interior was equally lavish. Such opulence! No wonder there was a revolution.

August 2008

ST. PETERSBURG
The sumptuous gardens of Peterhof Palace.

THAILAND

Tucked away in a quiet corner of Thailand, far from the gleaming palaces and traffic-choked streets of Bangkok, is the delightful town of Nan. There I encountered friendly people, few tourists, and a charming market selling food, both ready-to-cook and takeout. The latter included red ant maggots and hatchlings in bamboo leaves, the usual grasshoppers, and other assorted insects. A guide took me to the village of Heuy Yuak, meaning "stream by the banana tree," our base for a trek to local communities and forests.

On our first day of walking the guide found a man from the Mlabri tribe of nomadic hunter-gatherers. He was dressed in a loincloth and shirt, and was cutting bamboo for the villagers. He led us to his camp, a simple open-sided hut with a roof of bamboo leaves. Terribly shy, his wife and children ran away as we approached, but the man, who had a dreamy, childlike quality, stayed and talked. The Mlabri were called People of the Forest or Yellow Leaf People, because as soon as the leaves on their huts turn yellow, in only a few days to a week, they move on. The simplicity of their lives was extraordinary; they possessed only a few baskets, blankets, and a kettle. The handmade baskets were beautiful: rattan on the outside, bamboo on the inside, with a layer of leaves between for waterproofing. The rattan was in different shades of brown and exquisitely woven. The woman and her children returned, but remained timid and anxious, and yet curious. I felt lucky to meet this family, as they were soon leaving to hunt lizards and anteaters. When asked by the guide what gifts they would like from visitors, they responded they would be grateful for tobacco and pork fat.

I was privileged to have visited them. Since that time, due to deforestation, they have lost their nomadic lifestyle and are forced to live in settlements. They now make hammocks for a living.

February 1995

HUEY YUAK, NAN
A shy Mlabri woman with her children.

SINGAPORE

Singapore was cleaner and more regimented than I had anticipated. Devoid of the usual Asian bustle, the only sidewalk activity was the methodical flattening of cardboard boxes and soda cans for recycling. Street food stalls were confined to lively markets with boundless choices, including an array of desserts with names such as *Bubor ChaCha*. A trip around town revealed an ethnic melting pot. Strolling through neighborhoods I saw influences of colonial British, Western, Chinese, Indian and Malay cultures.

In the city center, elegant steel and glass skyscrapers dwarfed the Victorian-style Cricket Clubhouse. The gothic spire of the Anglican St. Andrew's Cathedral evoked Britain in a bygone era, as did Raffles Hotel, its arcades, balustrades and balconies all in perfect white. Little India, with its Hindu temples supporting a riot of animated deities on their roofs, had more of the hubbub of an Indian city. I enjoyed a tray of assorted curries without knowing exactly what everything was. At the Malabar Mosque in the Arab Street Quarter, tasteful in blue tile and golden dome, I closed my eyes at the call to prayer and was transported to the Middle East. Most Muslims here, however, are Malay or Indian. Tucked behind, the Kampong Glam Cemetery — the domain of Malay royalty ghosts — was a disarray of tombstones like ornate chess pawns. A few were lovingly dressed in yellow head-cloths.

At the Chinese *Temple of a Thousand Lights*, the back door of a fifteen-foot Buddha led inside the statue itself. In this chamber visitors caressed a small reclining Buddha with tenderness. His feet were thoughtfully cooled by a fan. At the Sunday Bird Market, tiny green birds hopped in tiny cages hung aloft in rows. Their Chinese owners engaged in enthusiastic bird discussions, eyes nearly always turned upward.

Interestingly, all these samples of the racial mix had retained their cultural or religious identity. Indeed the contents of the pot had not melted, rather mingled in a stew of ethnic flavors.

November 2000

KAMPONG GLAM CEMETERY
Tombstones adorned with head-cloths.

SPAIN

The Spanish are a civilized bunch, but periodically display behavior verging on the lunatic. The feast of Saint Sebastian in Palma is one such occasion.

As I entered the old town, the frenetic party had started in a plaza, with fireworks tumbling over an old stone arch floodlit with a fiery red glow. Through this gate marched bands of sinister figures, accompanied by drummers pounding a relentless primeval beat. They wore devil masks, helmets with horns, and flowing medieval clothes. They ran dementedly, thrusting flaming torches at bystanders. As the macabre procession continued through the streets, a new group emerged through the arch.

A man appeared pushing a cart adorned with animal skulls and spouting fireworks. Masked men hauled a tall scaffold with dangling devils, flares, and pyrotechnics pointing skywards. More demons appeared holding bicycle wheels on poles that spun with the force of ignited roman candles, showering fiery traces into the air. Hooded and masked youths ran under these wheels, jumping up and down to the drumbeat. Diving in myself, I felt a spark streak up my sleeve. By then the air was thick with acrid smoke, and yellow and white glitter; it pulsed with the incessant drumming. As the participants became more and more frenzied, I fully expected a virgin to be brought out for sacrifice. The highlight of the diabolical madness was a young man who burst forth with six blazing Roman candles in V-formation on his back. He weaved in and out of the crowd until his flowing robes caught fire and had to be extinguished, momentarily slowing him.

I followed the procession through Palma to the magnificent cathedral, suffused in red, where the finale was the ultimate in firework displays. Walking back through town, I was amused to see that the cleaning crews had already cleared up the demonic debris. It appeared that nothing out of the ordinary had happened at all.

January 2008

PALMA, MALLORCA
The smoke and glitter from fireworks silhouettes a masked man.

TURKEY

The bus to Kapıkırı was delayed while two people were still seeing the doctor, so I was ushered into a café and given tea. The drive to the village was dramatic, the bus weaving through a rock-strewn landscape dotted with castles. A mountain of huge boulders loomed over the village. Ahead, an old man slowly walked a donkey laden with a wife and several heavy sacks. The bus stopped and the load was put on board, including the wife.

I explored. Rural village life had evolved amongst Roman and Byzantine ruins, which were welded to rocks, incorporated into houses, and often delineated fields. A woman walked through her garden scattered with fluted columns. The village was perched on a lake. Mehmet, a boatman who spoke no English but was a master of communication through mime, took me on an afternoon float. We landed at an elegant, ruined medieval castle that rose like a magical Camelot in a natural line from its rocky island base.

The following morning, walking up a steep hill behind the village, I sought quiet solitude. My heart sank as an older woman followed me with a spring in her step and a bundle of textiles for sale under her arm. But she had a jolly face, a lovely smile, and the bundle stayed unopened. At the top of the hill, we stood together as the sun began to bathe the village and lake in a soft morning light. The lady, Durdu Yıldırım, spoke a little English and invited me to her house for tea. The upstairs living room of her modest dwelling had low seats covered with thick fabric, surrounding a Turkish carpet. She brought tea and sweet homemade flatbread and showed me photos of people who had stayed with her. Finally she opened her bale and laid out a variety of cloth. She watched my face and put aside the ones she knew I liked, a soft white headscarf and a geometric weaving of cream and blue. At home I look at these pieces and remember how Durdu welcomed me into her home.

July 2007

KAPIKIRI
A village garden strewn with Roman stonework.

IRAN

Never was a country more delightfully surprising than Iran. Feeling bold, I had swept aside negative popular opinion and media sensationalism and joined a tour group. I discovered a people who were intelligent, cultured, and who felt more connected to Europe and the West than to their Arab neighbors. They were also devastatingly good-looking!

In the holy city of Mashhad, I climbed to a rooftop restaurant. Without a guide I was unable to understand the Farsi menu, so I was invited into the kitchen to choose my food. There were the standard kebabs, but the chicken in sauce caught my eye. I pointed to it, but the waiter indicated it was only for him. Again I tried but again he said no. Finally, I plucked from my cerebral folds the Farsi word for please — *lotfan*. Amid laughter and smiles from the kitchen staff he relented. It was delicious. Through the restaurant window I could see the mosque buzzing with activity; the gold domes glowing in the night. The shrine was decorated in tiles and mosaics of exquisite beauty and outstanding craftsmanship, typical of many cultural and religious sites in Iran.

At the end of the trip I stayed with an Iranian family for a few days. They were charming and educated, and welcomed me into their home with a graciousness in which Muslims excel. The mother was curious about my life, other countries and customs, and engaged me in conversation through her two daughters, who were fluent in English. We found common ground with ease, especially in our humor. Hilarious stories were recounted and witty observations shared. Lavish feasts were prepared and I was chauffeured around Tehran to see the sights. They presented me with a beautiful wall hanging embroidered with gold thread and tiny pearls. My lingering memory is of the family at the airport security gate, waving goodbye with a sparkle in their eyes, radiating goodwill.

Iran had turned out to be wonderful; there was no need at all to feel bold.

September 2009

MASHHAD
The mosque, aglow at night, buzzes with activity.

CHILE

I liked Darwin immediately. As we drove across the desert he was calm and steady, pleasant and cheerful, spoke slowly so I could understand, and was infinitely patient when I didn't. The soft browns, pinks, and purples in the sculpted rocks soothed the hard, dry landscape. The village of Chiu Chiu stood, in muted shades of beige, above the cultivated Rio Loa valley. It appeared as an oasis of green patchwork fields in the bone-dry terrain.

Darwin and I strolled the streets. The adobe church built in 1611 dominated the plaza with its twin bell towers. Its thick walls sheltered a cool interior where the rafters were made of cactus wood. We sat in the quiet of the plaza shade, near the school with a thatched roof. Suddenly the calm was broken by a long line of excited children on bicycles, off for a jaunt. A few seconds later, with comedic timing, a girl appeared head down, furiously pedaling to catch up. A man guided his llamas and sheep over the river and up a hill, although they seemed to know where to go. Petroglyphs on the rock walls of the river valley depicted the same scene of shepherds and llamas. Those age-old traditions have continued to this day. These shy people lived in simple dwellings of adobe or rough stone with wooden doors and windows, and no electricity. In their yards were the distinctive domes of outdoor ovens. I stopped short at the sight of the cemetery. Simple wooden crosses were festooned with brightly colored paper flowers giving the place the cheerful look of a fiesta in those subdued surroundings.

Dropping me off at the bus stop for my onward journey, Darwin calmly informed me he was now driving to the hospital where his wife was due to give birth. I hope the baby didn't arrive early!

June 2011

CHIU CHIU
At the cemetery simple wooden crosses are festooned with brightly colored paper flowers.

KENYA

As the open-sided Mercedes truck lumbered along dirt roads, smaller safari vans were stuck at dizzy angles. Drivers and guides worked to free wheels from muddy quagmires. Later, the Little Tractor That Could had to extricate our truck too. It was unseasonably rainy and green, and not my expectation of Africa. But arriving in the Maasai Mara, the vista opened to classic savanna. Stunning valley views of grass, bush, or the occasional lone acacia tree were revealed between rounded hills. The brilliant red plaid wraps of the Maasai people punctuated this soft landscape.

In just a few hours I had viewed an impressive array of wildlife: impala, warthog, water buffalo, elephant, giraffe, and even a distant leopard. The highlight was seeing two sleepy lionesses, draped in a tree, tails dangling. I felt lucky to be so near.

A roadside lunch was prepared. As it was finishing, a young male lion sauntered out of the bush, heading directly for us. Was he looking for lunch himself? The guide barked orders to pack up NOW! Tables, chairs, dishes, and food were stowed in the truck in record time, the side door closing just as the lion arrived. He flopped in the shade next to the vehicle, so near that with a good stretch, I could have reached down and tousled his mane. I alternated between intense curiosity and shooting volleys of photos. At intervals he looked up, his penetrating amber eyes staring intently. His nose bore the scars of many battles. Simultaneously it was unnerving and enthralling. Eventually the truck had to depart and as the engine started he reluctantly rose and ambled directly to the shadow of a nearby van. So he didn't want to eat us after all, he just needed respite from the intense African sun.

February 2007

MAASAI MARA NATIONAL PARK
A battle-scarred lion gazes at the bus.

JORDAN

At sunrise I looked out at the soft Middle Eastern light bathing the houses of Amman. The pattern of squares and rectangles was like the fabric in a Klimt painting. As the bus climbed away from the city into the Gilead hills, I observed a landscape that appeared simultaneously hard and soft; it felt biblical in its rounded brown hillsides studded with yellow, red, and blue wildflowers and ancient rock terraces of olive and fruit trees. Stopping at a roadside stall I was cordially served a glass of fresh hot black tea poured over a sprig of mint. It was the most delicious tea I have ever tasted. Further on, a collection of low concrete buildings in bad condition, bristling with TV aerials and solar panels, comprised a Palestinian refugee camp.

It was thrilling to walk into the oval forum of the exceptional Roman city of Jerash. Unbroken marble columns ringed this vast paved marketplace. Equally breathtaking was the mostly intact amphitheater, where from a central stone on the stage the merest whisper could be heard in the uppermost benches. Locals came and went in Jerash, as if still inhabiting the city. A man carried a lamb, boys with heart-melting smiles sold chewing gum, and five gentlemen played an uproarious game of cards inside a superb carved stone basin.

At the magnificent Temple of Artemis, the tall columns were capped with lavish Corinthian capitals. The guide inserted a knife at the column base, and to my amazement the knife moved up and down as the column swayed imperceptibly. The most impressive structure was the Temple of Zeus, where the hardest of rock had been cut into blocks and columns with such precision that it was impossible to slip even a cigarette paper into the cracks. It was thought to have been faced originally with sandalwood and tiles from India. There was a mystery surrounding the stone. No one knows where it came from, how it was brought to the site, or how it was lifted into place. The enigma remains sealed as tightly as the joints in the masonry.

March 1990

JERASH
A game of cards in a Roman stone basin.

ICELAND

Iceland is a story of continuous formation and destruction. In fact, the whole country is a piece of performance art. I saw this geology in action, translated by nature into dramatic scenery; a thundering waterfall, an ash-caked glacier, a towering basalt cliff. There was great beauty in the geological structure, especially when I looked closely.

Icelanders have a strong bond with nature, but perhaps most of them don't realize it. Many artists tap into this connection and the Icelandic subconscious is a font of creativity, said to spring from the long hours of darkness in winter. This is particularly evident in architecture. The white church Hallgrímskirkja dominates the Reykjavik skyline. A concrete construction, its side wings of hexagonal columns swoop up to the bell tower spire. These geometric pillars echo the magnificent basalt columns to be found throughout Iceland and, in particular, the cliffs and caves of the south coast. This theme is continued in the newly completed Harpa, an impressive concert hall and convention center on the Reykjavik waterfront. The Icelandic-Danish artist Olafur Eliasson designed the façade and the ceiling as a honeycomb of hexagonal cells. This time the basalt is in cross section. Further connections with nature can be seen in the coal-gray color of the lobby, the indigo walls of the Northern Lights Hall, and the glowing red interior of the main auditorium, Eldborg, named after one of Iceland's volcanic craters.

Key in the design of the Harpa is the concept of multiple uses of space. I found this everywhere in Iceland, from the tiny guesthouse where the breakfast buffet was on a shelf projecting over a stairwell, to a sculpture installation in the underground caverns of a hydroelectric power station. For a nation of just over 300,000 people, such creativity, ingenuity, and inspiration is admirable.

June 2011

HARPA CONCERT HALL, REYKJAVIK
The honeycomb of glass cells echoes the pattern of the local basalt.

INDIA

"A thing of beauty is a joy forever."

The last thing I expected to hear from a vendor in Kashmir was a quote from Keats. But this was a perfect line to sell cashmere shawls so fine they could pass through a wedding ring. It was sublime salesmanship.

The sumptuous interiors of houseboats on the shores of Lake Nagin were constructed of wood with exquisitely carved pillars and panels. The floors were laden with thick maroon hand-woven carpets. Vendors arrived continuously. I sat sipping tea as a bewildering array of goods passed before me, accompanied by patient and good-natured — but persevering — sales techniques. I bought a delicate silver drinking bowl from a quiet exiled Tibetan lady. She and the bowl shared a past life, so very different from the present. The vendors arrived in slender wooden boats, *shikaras*, that are the main mode of travel in this watery community. My favorite was the flower-seller. Every day he filled his boat with an array of gorgeous blooms glowing in bright colors.

I took trips in *shikaras* on the tranquil lake, paddled quietly by a boatman, Ali, whose white skullcap graced his handsome angular face. Stopping at a floating garden, he plucked a lotus blossom the size of a dinner plate for me to hold. I felt like a *maharani*, a Hindu queen, as I reclined on pillows and took in the breathtaking beauty of the surroundings.

While politicians battle for control of Kashmir, the ethnic and religious mix didn't seem to be a problem for Kashmiris, many of whom had good friends of different religions. The one unifying trait they all had — more binding than any treaty or law — was their undying support of the Pakistani cricket team.

August 1989

LAKE NAGIN, KASHMIR
Gorgeous blooms fill the flower-seller's shikara.

JAPAN

The Japanese have a highly refined aesthetic sense; even the thermos at a youth hostel had a haiku on it:

Spring wind strokes the trees
And the blossoms laugh
Sending petals dancing

It had been an emotional day. I had taken the *Shinkansen* bullet train from Kyoto to Hiroshima. Riding the superb Japanese railway system, from the tiniest of trains (where I could sit in front next to the driver) to the speedy *Shinkansen*, I never had to wait more than twenty minutes for a train the entire trip. Making my way to the A-Bomb Dome, the iconic shell of a building in central Hiroshima, I found the site was filled with reminders of the violence of war. The delicately beautiful strings of origami cranes draped nearby evoked in me both sorrow for the past and the hope for peace.

To soothe my soul, I rode the ferry to Miyajima Island. Here was a tranquil temple, the Itsukushima Shrine and its Torii, a simple graceful gate, both painted in a striking orange. The shrine and gate stood in the tidal zone and appeared to be floating at high tide. A monk played a flute in a soft, atonal way, while a young couple quietly studied an egret that was poised motionless in the calm water. At sunset I wandered the temple terraces, following a path lighted with stone lanterns. The setting sun made the walls glow. I caught my breath as I passed a stone font and saw that the reflection of the temple had turned the water scarlet.

September 1991

ITSUKUSHIMA SHRINE, MIYAJIMA ISLAND
The reflection of the temple walls in the water of a drinking font.

ECUADOR

Touring the Galapagos Islands in the budget boat had its pros and cons. The small wooden vessel had character and creaked with a life of its own; but it leaked, we ran out of food, and my bunk was so cramped that in a fit of claustrophobia I fled to the roof, my sleeping place for the rest of the trip.

The wildlife was abundant and totally fearless. There were many favorites including exceedingly flaky and crusty marine iguanas, in assorted colors depending on what they ate, who swam by folding their limbs and waggling their tails. Male frigate birds made themselves attractive by inflating large red balloons at their throats. The careful courtship dance of the blue-footed booby was intriguing, the pair alternately raising and lowering their baby-blue paddles or spreading wings and pointing beaks skyward. The patient brown pelican, perching on a dinghy gunwale in the hope of a fishy morsel, balanced by flapping its feet like airplane ailerons. Upside-down fish shoaled around the hull of the boat. The iconic giant tortoise's speed belied its astonishing size. No wonder Darwin was profoundly inspired here.

But most of all I loved the sea lions, lounging on the beach calling, snorting and scratching, and constantly adjusting and maneuvering to get just a little more comfortable and attain maximum body contact with neighbors. These creatures were most graceful in the water, the pups playing, cavorting, and porpoising, and never missing the opportunity to swim with a boat. It was a joyful experience to snorkel with these juveniles and to join in with the pirouettes of their underwater ballet. They would roll, turn and dive with effortless agility and panache, chasing air bubbles or playing ball using sea urchins. How wonderful to spend all one's juvenile life having a good time.

April 1992

GALAPAGOS ISLANDS
A young sea lion snoozes.

GUATEMALA

Walking in the evening, through the colonnades of the elegant plaza, I encountered the bodies of sleeping traders, ready with their goods for market the next day. I was in the colonial town of Antigua, the gem of Guatemala. At one end of the plaza stood the ornate Baroque cathedral. Looking up from here, the heart of the city, one can see it is completely surrounded by volcanoes and mountains, rising green and majestic into the mists. In the town, many of the ancient churches were in ruins from a lineage of earthquakes. Many crumbling interiors were visible behind wrought-iron gates.

I ate breakfast in the tranquil and sheltered courtyard of a former convent. White arches spanned yellow ochre walls, adorned with hanging baskets and climbing shrubs. The greenery was accentuated by splashes of red, magenta, and bright orange flowers. At the market, the traders had set up their clothing, bags, and rugs famous to Guatemala. The textiles in vivid hues were visually stunning. An old woman, wearing traditional dress, sat on the floor surrounded by her wares. The women of a particular place all wear the same costume identifying their home village.

On a trip to Santa Maria, I boarded the bus and stopped cold. The entire vehicle was filled with women and girls, all wearing the same striking clothes. In a sea of color, headscarves, bodices and skirts were of the most incredibly rich blue. They were murmuring quietly in their native Mayan dialect. Having come from the market, the women held large bundles of green aromatic herbs, the scent filling the whole bus. Sitting down amidst this colorful mass of humanity, I breathed in every moment of it. It was a feast for the senses.

November 1993

ANTIGUA
A woman in traditional dress surrounded by her wares.

NEPAL

With a day to spare in Kathmandu, fellow traveler David and I sought adventure. With luck we found a young man kind enough to lend us his Royal Enfield motorbike. With a blissful look he described the riding experience on his machine as "a different kind of joy." David expertly negotiated Kathmandu traffic, particularly on the insane Ring Road, using a "go with the flow" technique.

Soon we climbed out of the city into a green landscape of terraced rice fields and hills carpeted with shrubs and trees. Clustered along the route were brick houses festooned with strings of chilies, and maize or grains drying on tarps spread on patios. Turning off the main road to the village of Chobhar, we headed for the temple to see the pots and pans nailed to the walls by hopeful newlyweds. To our surprise and delight we came upon an animated scene in the temple courtyard. Rows of women in colorful clothes were each seated in front of a yellow paper mandala. At the direction of two men bedecked in gold, they would place items from an adjacent brass tray onto the paper: a pinch of powder, a little popcorn, small flowers, some gray mud, a white tassel. There was a festive atmosphere; the women were clearly delighted to be participating. Only the black dog lying by the steps was dreaming in another world, his reluctant departure prompted by a gentle sprinkling of holy water.

Our splendid day discovering the area continued on the Enfield until we returned the trusty steed to its owner. He would not take any compensation; a full tank and a clean bike were more than adequate. It seems in Nepal the reverence for the Royal Enfield is instilled at an early age. Earlier in the day we had parked at an overlook. I glanced back to see a file of school children walk past the bike, each affectionately patting the seat.

September 2006

CHOBHAR
Women enjoying a Hindu ritual.

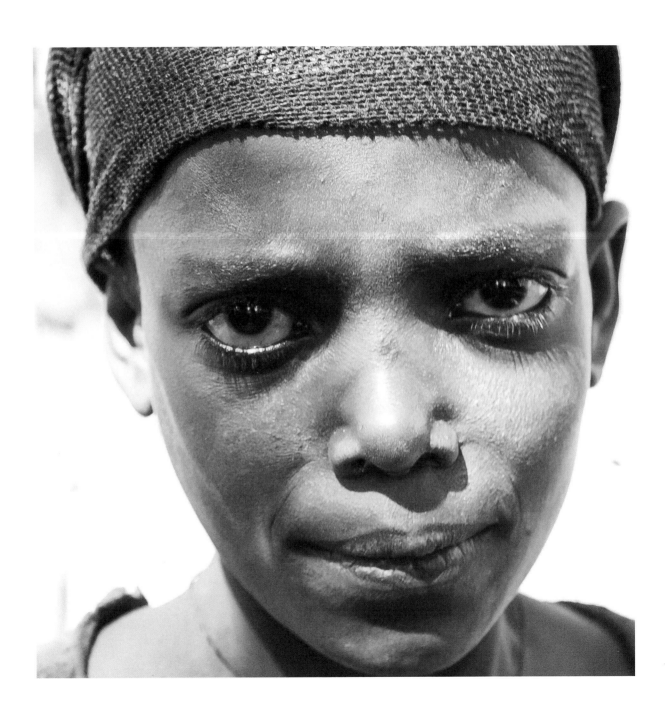

ETHIOPIA

Crunching along on stubble and stone, I repeatedly came to abrupt breaks in the earth's crust. The land dropped away to steep-sided chasms plunging to the silver or brown threads of rivers thousands of feet below. I was in Ethiopia, the unique gem of Africa that is home to hundreds of Grand Canyons. On this four-day guided walk, we meandered through village and farm, staying at specially constructed round huts or *tukuls*. In this enterprise, community members are employed and the proceeds directly benefit the participating villages. The *tukuls* were modest but comfortable, and the toilet hut had no door, providing a stupendous view.

We visited the country's distinctive Orthodox churches in groves of mature olive trees. The brightly daubed eaves of the plain circular exteriors mirrored the riot of color and exuberance of the paintings on the walls of the inner sanctum. Compositions in the linear Orthodox style included diverse biblical scenes alongside the patron Saint George on a white stallion dispatching a dragon or two. The priest began chanting sonorously in the ancient language *Ge'ez*, and I felt I might have been back in the time when the Christian church had just awakened.

Each day I met people smiling, welcoming, calm, quiet and gentle. Abandoning a sheep or goat, children would appear from nowhere, many wearing clothes of green, the color of hope. Pleased to see me, but too shy to speak, they would firmly shake my hand, which I gladly reciprocated, disregarding a runny nose or infected eye. I noticed a girl in whose penetrating gaze I could read a deep sorrow. I can only dream that some day she would find hope as green as the color of her frayed dress.

January 2007

KORA ANBESSA
The young girl with sorrowful eyes.

FRENCH POLYNESIA

On the midnight approach to Tahiti, the sea was so calm I could see the reflection of the stars upon it. The sails were lowered and the engine switched on. I lay on the bow, looking at a plume of bioluminescence in a green arc from the hull. In an amazing display, sparks like electrical discharges were shooting away in strings, constantly changing and tumbling. It was a riot of motion in emerald light on the black water.

I was hitchhiking across the South Pacific on sailboats, starting in Panama and ending in Tonga. Six months of no shoes and little clothing. Tahiti was a most spectacular port of call, with its green cliffs and craggy peaks. In Papeete Harbor, a canoe regatta showcased bronzed powerhouses, heads bowed, paddling their slivers of boats balanced by outriggers.

When traveling, mundane events turn into unexpected encounters. At the launderette the French owners, who had sailed from France and stayed ever since, gave me a complimentary beer. A trip to the post office turned into a memorable experience when I came across a large gathering of Polynesians dancing and singing in traditional dress. I squeezed to the front for an exceptional view of beautiful women, with remarkably long black hair, in grass skirts with tassels, coconut shell bras, and feathered headdresses. The men were similarly dressed but with no need for the coconuts. Others, more soberly attired in long white dresses with high collars for the ladies, or shirts and pants for the men, were earnestly singing religious songs. This was in sharp contrast to the scantily clad, with their suggestive hip-swiveling dances. The sacred and the sensual.

June 1992

PAPEETE, TAHITI
Gorgeous Polynesian dancers in traditional costume.

INDONESIA

Surely there cannot be a more culturally diverse country than Indonesia. In a graceful crescent from Indian to Pacific oceans, more than 17,000 islands are home to very contrasting peoples, from the devout Muslims of northern Sumatra to the indigenous animists in Papua. A lucid thread, the national language of *Bahasa Indonesia*, links the nation's 300-plus ethnic groups. Aptly, the country's motto is "Unity Through Diversity."

Before successive visitors left their religious impressions, the inhabitants were animist. Some communities have staved off conversion pressures and remain animist today. In their belief there is no boundary between the spiritual and physical world; everything has a soul. Visiting one such village, Boti in Timor, I found the difference in attitude to life palpable. Set in beautiful gardens named Land of the Birds, the plants, as an age-old tradition, had been grown synergistically, and all had a function: edible, medicinal, or for construction, dyeing or weaving. Birds are revered and protected for their value in processing seeds to make stronger seedlings. I met Sau, the King's niece, who was dressed in handmade clothes. She sat with grace and poise making cordial conversation with a calm assuredness. Like the other villagers she had no sense of her age, because birth certificates are not issued. Their calendar is based on a nine-day week, and for each day thinking is focused on one aspect of society, such as children day, nature day or even "do your best" day!

What is most remarkable is the lack of fines, punishments or prisons. If a man steals, the transgressor admits his guilt at an interview with the King. Upon returning to the village he will be given more of what he stole by the community. It is interesting to speculate what the rest of the world would be like with such a system!

May 2012

BOTI, TIMOR
The poise and grace of Sau, the King's niece.

BOTSWANA

In Botswana I learned to take my time, to be polite. Commencing a conversation, however simple, I remembered to greet Botswanans with "*Dumela*," followed by "How are you?" I knew to wait for a measured reply. A beam of pleasure would appear on the faces of these proud and independent people when I held my left hand under my right wrist while shaking hands, or touched the inside of my right forearm with the straight fingers of my left hand when giving or receiving.

I was on safari in a Namibian rental car that was slowly being ruined. I saw birds with wonderful names such as lizard buzzard, grassveld pipit, red-faced mousebird, Swainson's francolin, helmeted guineafowl, bateleur, Egyptian goose, long-tailed paradise whydah, red-winged pratincole, and lastly the spotted dikkop.

On boat rides along the Chobe River I observed outstanding wildlife. Large, gray, floating bumps transformed into hippos that were yawning, grunting, grumbling and groaning. A lioness dragged the limp body of a kudu (antelope) under a bush, allowing her cubs to eat undisturbed. A herd of sleek impala, nervously supervised by the dominant male, in precarious command, approached to drink. Juvenile baboons, overseen by a portly female, played and tumbled like toddlers. I witnessed an astonishing struggle between a water monitor (a four-foot-long lizard) and a leopard. The monitor lashed out with its talons, the leopard dodged and slashed with its claws. Finally the leopard lunged, biting the monitor's throat and clenching tight until its adversary went limp. The lizard had fought gamely, but the leopard prevailed with its strength and agility.

A mature male giraffe drank at the river's edge, legs splayed wide. Superb physiological adaptations allow his head to descend from what seemed like the stratosphere without pressure-washing his brain. At the end of the trip I returned the battered rental car in Namibia in a sorry state. It needed much more than a pressure-wash.

April 2004

CHOBE
A male giraffe takes a drink.

SYRIA

Touring Syria is like taking a walk through civilization since prehistory. I was treated to: twelfth-century Crusader castles, Bronze Age sites, an Arab-Christian Basilica from 400 A.D., thirteenth-century Mamluk bathhouses, archaeological sites from 5000 B.C., and the Road to Damascus where Saint Paul was converted. The crowning glory, with its signature palm-shaped capitals, was Palmyra, the colony usurped from the Roman Empire by Queen Zenobia, a descendant of Cleopatra. I saw villages where only Aramaic, the ancient language of the Bible, is spoken. Visiting historians must think they are in paradise.

Apricot and olive trees and the small, white flowers of the mulberry bushes accentuated the terrain, while the scent of orange blossoms filled the air. Charming villages like Job Mady featured houses made of wattle and daub; some were square, some beehive-shaped, many with delightful courtyards. I came across a small group of people resting quietly on a shaded mat. They were friendly and gracious, and enjoyed my effort to speak Arabic. A patriarch, with his grandchild neatly perched in his lap, posed with dignity and a little sparkle in his eye.

At times, as in any Muslim country, the early morning call to prayer was not welcome; the quality of the voices varied. Some, however, were sublime, providing a celestial wake-up call. I was on the top terrace of the Muslim castle at Aleppo, enjoying the dramatic view of the city rooftops. Suddenly a thousand calls to evening prayer burst out over the whole city in a most remarkable sound. Voices, one piled on top of the other, vied for ascendancy with rising and falling tones, like a tuning orchestra. I stood with my eyes closed taking in this music that sent a tingle down my spine.

March 2001

JOB MADY
A village patriarch and his grandson.

COOK ISLANDS

As each wall of water towered before me, I wondered if I would survive. But in an instant, the little sailboat was on top of the wave and a second later its frothing crest would rush away into the night. The vessel was only thirty feet long in this roiling ocean, but she was steel and she was sturdy. The captain and I had hoisted a handkerchief-sized storm jib to maintain our heading, so there was nothing left but to go below, secure the main hatch and listen to Vivaldi. Four days later the tempest subsided as quickly as it had commenced, and we limped somewhat bruised and battered into the atoll of Aitutaki.

The Cook Islands were not as wealthy or manicured as French Polynesia, but the warm and friendly people had pleasant smiles and New Zealand accents. A man showed me the full-sized replica of a double wooden canoe sailed by his grandfather from Hawaii. Constructed using rope and wooden pegs, it was carved with designs depicting peace, including overlapping broken arrows and stylized figures holding hands. Wandering further I found the plump ladies of the Apostolic Church sitting happily, chatting and weaving panels of coconut palm leaves. They spoke of their children who had migrated to New Zealand for job opportunities, but who couldn't afford to come back. If they were able to return they could subsist and work small jobs, to have a better life at home.

It is unusual to see a rugby field surrounded by palm trees, but the standard of the play was impressively high for such a small population. The atmosphere, however, was informal; a hen and her chicks ventured onto the playing area several times, the referees padded up and down in flip flops, and at the end, people drove their motorbikes across the grass to take the shortcut home. Most refreshing of all was the spectators' reaction to the game, falling about in hoots of good-natured laughter at the slightest fumble or other mistake. After all, it is only a game, isn't it!

June 1992

AITUTAKI
Team talk at a rugby match.

CHINA

Such a land of paradox is China, that for much of the time I was on an emotional and intellectual seesaw. When I thought I was starting to understand the country, another experience turned that notion upside down.

I soon learned that the word *meo* means don't have, can't, there isn't, or just plain no, and yet many people welcomed me and showed great kindness. Beautiful and impressive sites like restored Buddhist temples or the Great Wall contrasted with litter-strewn surroundings and the most unsanitary public toilets I have ever seen. Cheap plastic kitsch was sold alongside exquisite silks and river pearls. A thick white nebula of pollution often obscured modern skyscrapers with innovative designs. I tasted a variety of truly delicious food, only to balk at a menu that included stewed bear paw.

In the main square of Chengdu stood a statue of Mao, right arm raised in fatherly guidance. In front was a lawn and behind a large advertising billboard, neither of which would have been permitted in his day. Relaxing in a teahouse bamboo chair, I gazed at a lake from under a willow tree and sipped delicious jasmine tea. A rat at the water's edge inspected a discarded plastic bag and, deeming the contents suitable, picked up the handle with its teeth and scurried away. Once banned in the Cultural Revolution, the teahouses were a newfound pleasure. People sat and chatted, or slept … or had their ears cleaned. I saw an ear-picker in action at the teahouse of the Wenshu Monastery using an alarming array of long metal instruments, including a mysterious one with fluffy white feathers. Concentrating, he stared into the distance, while his client — quite unperturbed — read a newspaper. To him it was clearly nothing, but to my Western eye it was both remarkable and scary to see one man's complete trust in another.

May 1999

WENSHU MONASTERY, CHENGDU
An ear-picker at the monastery teahouse.

UNITED KINGDOM

The vibrant, cosmopolitan city of London is home to world-class art museums. Since the nineteenth century the Tate Museum has been at the forefront of controversy in the art world, particularly causing a stir in the '70s with an infamous exhibit of a stack of bricks. The Tate Modern, London's most visited, is ingeniously housed in a converted power station on the south bank of the River Thames. The exhibition space (whilst not as graceful as the Musée D'Orsay, a converted train station in Paris) lends itself perfectly to the modern and contemporary art on display. Its lines are clean, simple and functional. The former turbine hall, of cathedral proportions, regularly houses massive installations.

In the museum café contemplating a cappuccino, I glanced up to see a split screen offering two windows on life. My table was placed directly opposite a thin glass partition separating the café from the kitchen. On the left was an animated scene: customers chatting, laughing, drinking, eating, and coming and going, with all the liveliness of humanity relaxed and enjoying themselves. On the right was a lone kitchen worker, walking with deliberation, a roll of paper towels under his arm. I was struck by the contrast before me.

It was interesting that the café patrons were completely oblivious to him; but he was very aware of them, and yet simultaneously in his own space. It would be easy to make judgments about the haves and have-nots in this world but who knows the roles played in any of these lives? One can only speculate.

October 2005

TATE MODERN, LONDON
Two windows on life.

CHILE

Flying west over the Pacific Ocean I wondered if I had been wise. Within hours of arriving in Chile I had impulsively bought a half-price ticket to Rapa Nui — the catch being I had to stay for a week. How would I fill the time on this tiny island? However, renting a jeep and armed with a map I explored remote places, bumping down rocky tracks, getting stuck in mud and stranded with a flat tire. Covering the remainder on foot or hitchhiking, I saw everything, often two or three times. Climbing to the top of Rano Kau, one of the isle's numerous volcanic craters, I gazed at 360 degrees of water on the horizon. The gently arcing curvature of the earth confirmed I was on "The Navel of the World," the lone dot in the center of the South Pacific Ocean. This theme is represented in such artistic renditions as a rough circular wall surrounding a beautifully smooth oval rock, or the small carved circles just above the elongated fingers of the *moai*, the island's iconic stone statues.

Moai can be seen everywhere on Rapa Nui as singles or in rows. The quarry, where many statues are unfinished, fascinated me as I could easily have stumbled over a stone nose or body. Their elongated faces with distinctive features, sunken eyes, curving noses and pouting lips were intriguing and captivating. Some had a hat of a different type of reddish stone representing the topknot of the male hairstyle. The statues were discovered toppled, a consequence of a vicious civil war. Their creators' demise is quite a mystery, but anthropologists and historians conclude that it was exacerbated by, amongst other things, population pressures and resource depletion. I wonder what lesson we could learn from this?

November 1997

RAPA NUI (EASTER ISLAND)
A row of enigmatic moai.

MONGOLIA

There was a buzz of high excitement in Ulaanbaatar; *Naadam* had begun. The Festival of the Three Manly Sports, Mongolia's most popular event, commenced in the National Stadium with impassioned speeches and a colorful pageant of ceremonial horsemen, girl contortionists, musicians and dancers. During the wrestling, the most beloved sport in Mongolia, the atmosphere was electric. The scantily dressed competitors enacted elaborate movements full of ritual and symbolism, flapping their arms like an eagle before and after rounds. The bouts involved minutes of impasse between locked adversaries and ended in an explosive burst of action bringing one man down, to the wild applause of the frenzied crowd.

On a course outside the city, where families picnicked and kites flew, I watched the second manly sport, horse racing. "Manly" is something of a misnomer; the jockeys were aged between five and thirteen, their light weight and lack of saddles increasing the horses' speed. The contestants and their mounts walked out to the start early in the morning, racing the twelve grueling miles back. Both rider and horse were exhausted at the end, but it didn't prevent an exciting finish when the horse in second place sprinted ahead of the leader at the winning post. The crowd went mad, the men yelling "*Cor, cor, cor*" as special encouragement.

The third part of *Naadam* was the archery competition, which was a spectacle in itself. The archers wore the traditional dress of a colorful robe and pointed hat. One splendid fellow in red could have been Genghis Khan himself. They held their composite bows in a measured meditation before shooting at a pyramid of small leather cylinders. Upon completion of each shot, officials would sing a beautiful haunting song to honor the contestant. Women also competed, implicitly trusting the men as they stood fifty feet in front of them, arrows whistling over their heads. These are brave women indeed, and perhaps the braver in this manly sport!

July 2008

NAADAM, ULAANBAATAR
An archer competes at a festival.

AUSTRALIA

It was hard to comprehend the vastness of Australia. Having spent days in vehicles, simply staring out the window at miles and miles of bush on endless roads, it soon became clear how uninhabited and enormous the country was. Thousands of acres would be under the domain of a small group of people living in astonishing isolation on a single homestead.

I came to love the outback's scrubby eucalyptus trees and buff-colored grasses, and its reddest of earth. A paved road was a black stripe on a rust background. Dust could be tasted when passing vehicles kicked up the dirt roads. Visibility decreased to nearly zero. Road trains, the trucks pulling trailers up to 160 feet long, hogged the highway and left the occasional pancaked cow or kangaroo. Drivers had to venture off-road to overtake the train.

It was worthwhile to get out and walk a little. I realized that, close up, the desert was alive with enterprise, including workaholic ants with green abdomens (that tasted of citrus) and termites constructing huge mounds with the ingenuity and expertise of civil engineers.

There is a good reason why cultural landmarks become so, and the monolith Uluru (Ayres Rock) is no exception. It really did turn brick red at sunset, and indeed I had a hard time taking my eyes off it at any time of day. Walking to the top at dawn, I reveled in the rock's sine waves, honeycombs and perforations. However, it was just after sunrise that I looked out from this spiritual spot and saw the pattern of a line and circle in the earth that held an extraordinary abstract beauty. It was this otherworldly landscape that impressed me most about the outback. It served too as a reminder that landmarks may captivate the visitor, but it also pays to look about you.

June 1994

ULURU-KATA TJUTA NATIONAL PARK
A pattern in the terrain.

LIBYA

With a barely audible patter, a dark figure turned into the passage ahead, robes floating gracefully. Receding arches framed the fleeting apparition as he disappeared into the shadows. The silence returned. In the wall above, a handprint was impressed in the whitewashed plaster; the Hand of Fatima is a symbol of protection against evil. The walls also featured spade-shaped lantern niches. The main thoroughfare broadened occasionally, making room for stucco benches draped with woven fabrics. Narrower, darkened side alleys could only be explored by flashlight.

Shafts of sunlight from wind towers pierced the gloom. These ingenious rectangular chimneys provide passive cooling, dramatically reducing the inside temperature. Large open plazas, one or two in each city quarter, often incorporated original Roman columns. Clever engineering brought spring water to all parts of the town, distribution strictly controlled by custodians.

House interiors were amazing. In the principal chamber and stairways the walls were painted with ornate red filigree designs, which also bordered mirrors and doors, such that little white remained. The lower walls were lined with cupboards, also highly decorated, and rich textiles covered the remaining wall space. Bedrooms were hidden behind dark green carved wooden doors and a small curtained alcove was used only for honeymooners or a widow's retreat. The flat roofs were the domain of women and housed the kitchens and, up there, the walkway between houses was for the exclusive use of females.

Urban planning was dictated by the social and economic life of the inhabitants. For all this and more, the ancient city of Ghadames was awarded UNESCO World Heritage status. But the town is now deserted, used only for prayer and during Ramadan. The inhabitants have moved to nearby accommodations with the conveniences of modern kitchens and flush toilets.

October 2005

GHADAMES
A solitary figure disappears into the shadows.

CAMBODIA

As I crossed the border, the officials changed from truculent Vietnamese to gentle Cambodian. I immediately sensed a nation still in shock from the horrifying regime of the Khmer Rouge. The country had an empty feeling; the people were subdued and forlorn. Each person I met had lost at least one family member.

As I entered Cambodia, the landscape changed from green to brown; the dry and dusty rice fields were fallow. At Lake Tonlé Sap the bland beige of the earth merged into the muddy water, like an endless flat desert. People were living on the lake in huddles of stilt houses, using boats as we do motorcars. A small boat with a rusty machine gun at the bow was transporting me to Siem Riep, the gateway to Angkor Wat. The water was churned to a chocolate froth by the props of two powerful outboards.

The temple complex of Angkor Wat is a Southeast Asian treasure. The many and varied Hindu and Buddhist temples are characterized by ornate towers and a marvel of bas-relief carving. Chauffeured by a young man named Theary, it took us three full days to tour the area on his motorbike-taxi.

In the Siem Riep telephone office everyone was intensely crocheting, including the manager. The victim of a land mine, many of which were still unexploded, the man had an artificial leg. On his prosthetic foot, the molded space between the big and second toes held his flip-flop strap. Later in Phnom Penh, sitting at a café table, I was continuously asked for money by a stream of men missing limbs or with other injuries. If I had given to all who approached I would quickly have run out of funds. Most upsetting was their sadness and the hopelessness of the situation; begging was their only source of income.

June 1999

TONLÉ SAP
Departing for Angkor Wat.

ANTARCTICA

Antarctica's isolation presents an adventure just to arrive. After flying the length of South America to Ushuaia in southern Argentina, I boarded the Russian icebreaker Akademik Shuleykin. We heaved in mountainous seas during the two-day crossing of Drake's Passage, while wandering albatross flew in constant easeful motion around the ship.

The spectacular scenery and wildlife of the Antarctic Peninsula, along with its history of whaling, exploration, and scientific bases, comprised a special sojourn. I was awestruck. From a towering cliff of ice, a chunk the size of a mansion crashed into the water, sending a giant wave surging ahead of frozen floating fragments. Viewed from a small boat, two sleeping humpback whales gently rolled from side to side, with an occasional blow. Icebergs of fabulous shapes were tinted with the deepest turquoise imaginable. Gargantuan elephant seals, resembling boulders, dozed on a beach.

The shell of a single-engine Otter plane, and the metal debris of whaling operations from a heroic age, lay on the steamy volcanic sands of Deception Island.

These chinstrap penguin chicks, organized into crèches by guardian adults, stood patiently waiting for parents to return with tasty morsels. When I perched quietly at the edge of the nursery, inquisitive juveniles approached and gently pecked my outer garments. The return of a parent brought comical chaos, as phony offspring claimed rights to dinner. The chick most persistent in the ensuing chase was deemed by the parent to be the true and deserving recipient of the catch of the day.

In the expertly crafted Antarctic Treaty, participating countries agreed to keep Antarctica free of commercial exploitation. Hopefully the world's last pristine continent will remain that way.

February 1997

ANTARCTIC PENINSULA
Chinstrap penguin chicks wait patiently.

MEXICO

Taking guidebook advice verbatim can sometimes be ill advised. Stepping off the bus in Felipe, it was soon clear that "steeped in history" was an optimistic description. Purchasing an onward bus ticket for Tulum, I wandered the town to alleviate the two-hour wait. The poor selection in the bakery was mitigated by the entertainment provided by daytime TV, characterized by a universal similarity.

I wandered to the shady plaza and settled in for the wait. Small-town life surrounded me. A man was painting the church a bright yellow with a roller on an incredibly long pole. The men repairing the plaza pavers called to me in the way only workmen do. A woman, ignoring the other empty benches, sat next to me, her kindly face framed with hair in curlers secured by a scarf. Her lack of English did not deter her from making a great effort to welcome and talk to me. She introduced me to her husband, whose main concern was my marital status, but who had to agree that husbands were indeed "*muchos problemas.*" They departed amidst profuse goodbyes, *encantadas* and a lingering waft of setting lotion.

Across the street, an elderly man shuffled slowly, stopping frequently to inspect small details in the sidewalk, the wall, the door. Crossing to the plaza, he sat and stared intently at his hand. I discreetly photographed him, hoping to get a natural shot, wondering if he'd noticed. Looking up, he came to sit next to me, and we began conversing, I with my best Spanglish and he with no teeth. Neither of us understood a word but it didn't matter. He let me take a portrait in which his eyes told the story of a life long lived. The two hours passed in an instant and it was time to go. By then, I was sorry to leave Felipe.

December 1990

FELIPE CARRILLO PUERTO
My companion in the plaza.

MALAYSIA

At two in the morning I stepped out of the mountain lodge into a night black beyond imagination. The sky was ablaze with stars girdled by a misty Milky Way. I started the final push for the summit, still very tired from the day before. That climb from Kinabalu Park Headquarters to the Laban Rata rest house had taken me seven hours. It had been bright and sunny, and I was entertained along the way by lush flora, including the smallest orchid in Southeast Asia and the tiniest pitcher plant in the world. The inflorescence of a spiny-stemmed rattan plant arched over five species of moss jostling for space in one small clump. Exquisite flowers lined the path, while wild raspberries lingered just out of reach. I was passed by nimble porters with skyscraper packs, the prize being awarded to the man in yellow with a seventy-seven-pound load.

The steps were very steep and took their toll on my muscles and joints. Reaching the rest house had seemed a sufficient feat, but more punishment lay ahead. On the push to the top, the track became so steep that in some places I hauled myself up on ropes. At 13,000 feet my breathing was labored despite frequent stops. As dawn arrived the strings of pearls (headlamps of climbers above and below) faded, revealing the bizarre shapes of weathered granite comprising the dogtooth summit. At the peak I found a perch and watched the sun rise, outlining nearby clouds in yellow and gold. I turned to look behind me. To my astonishment, the sun had cast a shadow of the mountain over the South China Sea in the shape of a black pyramid, transporting me back to Egypt.

It was a long, cruel tramp down the mountain, the high-cut steps jarring every bone and muscle. I stumbled through the entrance gate having taken seventeen hours to complete the entire climb. I glanced up at a notice board showing the results of the 2009 Kinabalu Climbathon. A Spaniard had completed the same route in two hours and forty-four minutes.

February 2010

MOUNT KINABALU, BORNEO
The shadow of Mt. Kinabalu on the South China Sea.

BELIZE

Of all the countries I have visited, I used to announce, Belize is the one I would not return to. Lodged in my memory were images of unfriendly locals: tall scary men trying to extort money, an incensed border official exploding with rage over a minor lapse in protocol, or a woman beating fighting dogs with a plank of wood. Belize City was so dangerous that around town, only a small amount of cash was put in a pocket and any other absolute essentials hidden inside a brown paper lunch bag. I had no good memories.

I was encouraged to write to give a balanced view of the world, and upon rereading my journal I was surprised to find many positive, but forgotten, narratives. At Bullet Tree Falls, the luminescent green orbs of fireflies danced in a darkened hotel room, which was perched in the crook of a guanacaste tree decorated with epiphytes. An old woman in San Ignacio sang to her parrots, who sang back, making it hard to tell who was performing. The ubiquitous use of cheerful blue and turquoise in Punta Gorda transformed dreary shacks and huts. A woman with matching hair curlers hung out laundry in these complementary colors.

Lying on the wooden jetty at Tobacco Cay, I saw faint stars in a hazy sky through the serrated fronds of the thatched roof. These gems mirrored points of phosphorescence in the water, which flashed and died in an instant. Proud Captain Buck with his barrel chest and beer in hand had transported me there to Reef End Lodge, where I was the only guest. The kind elderly proprietor sat down with me during meals and told stories of the Cays and their folk, usually involving some sort of impropriety.

It is an interesting human characteristic that my mind clung to the negative experiences of Belize and lost the positive ones. Indeed it is worth remembering that there are good souls in every corner of this world.

December 1994

PUNTA GORDA
A woman's curlers match her surroundings.

MYANMAR

I traveled off the beaten track in a country that was off the beaten track. It wasn't easy. The toot of a minibus woke me one day at four in the morning when I should have been in it. Scrambling out of bed, I grabbed my belongings, ran out of the hotel and flew on board the bus. Three generations and I were crammed together in one seat. The body heat was welcome. The bus collected more people, drove around the corner — and stopped for breakfast. Setting off again at a crawl it was clear that something was wrong. We all pushed the van up a hill, but after anxiously peering at the engine, the driver announced that the vehicle "didn't like the Austrian lady sitting on the roof." With no solution in sight, I transferred to the last available place in a taxi, in the trunk.

At Kalaw I trekked into native villages with an Anglo-Indian named George. As we entered the Pa-O community of Le-in-go, a swarm of excited children hurtled towards us including a little fellow propelling himself on a cart. The place was very clean; only scattered cow pies were to be avoided. Wooden dwellings on stilts consisted only of two rooms. We visited an older woman with a brown, wrinkled face, wearing the traditional dress of a black sarong, a short black tunic and a turban. I was offered a delicious meal of nut-flavored red rice, curried cabbage, and a soup with ginger and peanuts. A bowl of water was presented to wash my hands before I ate the food with my fingers. She cooked on an open fire in a wooden tray of ashes set into a yielding bamboo floor. There were very few possessions: a thin mattress, hollow gourds hanging from a rack above the fire, and a large wooden Buddhist shrine with flowers.

We visited another elderly woman, who was amazed I was there. "Why have you come to Myanmar?" she asked. Momentarily dumfounded, I thought to reply with the age-old answer, "Because it's there."

January 1995

LE-IN-GO
A swarm of excited children hurtles towards me.

SOUTH AFRICA

Think of South Africa, and images of kids playing soccer on dusty township streets, or big game roaming the savanna come to mind. Indeed, the wildlife superstars of the national parks to the north more than meet expectations. But many people are unaware of how dramatically scenic and green the temperate South can be.

Exploring the spectacular Garden Route, I drove winding roads up steep, wild, and wooded V-shaped valleys of lush forest vegetation. Waterfalls the color of black tea nursed riotous plant life. A tumble of arum lilies in a gully made its own verdant cascade. Fast flowing rivers ran through deep gorges and, reaching the ocean at the rocky coastline, met rollers crashing onto the beach with relentless force. Further west, fishing villages with little wooden boats were centered on sweet harbors. In larger towns, like Stellenbosch, custodians in costume presented quaint white Dutch-style houses with squeaky floorboards and furniture from the colonial period. Here too were vineyards producing world-class wines. Table Mountain's mesa provided a different terrain from the cosmopolitan city of Cape Town below, dramatized further by the glimpse through the narrow Platteklip Gorge. Also here was the view of Camps Bay, said to be the most beautiful beach in the world.

I never met any boys playing soccer on dusty township streets. Even though Apartheid had ended two years earlier, the townships were still no-go areas for tourists. Zipping past on the highway, I saw people living in miserable conditions in dark and dismal wooden shacks. I had little meaningful interaction with black South Africans; those in service jobs were just about the only contact. These folks were quiet and subdued. The window to the Black Soul was closed. I left South Africa with wonderful memories of the gorgeous landscape and amazing wildlife, but with little insight into the mind of the majority of the people.

October 1996

STORMS RIVER MOUTH
Surf batters the rugged coast of the Garden Route.

TAIWAN

"What am I doing here?" was the question chiming in my head. Taipei in the gloom was noisy, jammed with traffic, and had shabby buildings covered in black mold from the humid polluted air. Escaping the city in search of the beautiful, I circumnavigated the island. A few gems could be found between dismal towns. Contorted rocks traced the wave-punished east coast. Monumental cliffs were sliced by a gray frothing river at Taroko Gorge. The sea that skirted the mountain Alishan was of clouds, not water.

For a small donation I stayed at a monastery in Fokuangshan. Nuns with black robes and shaved heads walked the halls with calm purpose. In the glow of evening candlelight, melodious, rhythmic chanting transported me to a higher plane. I felt at peace. When I left, a nun pressed a pink enamel brooch into my palm for good luck. Its heart shape framed the Chinese phrase "As one wishes." That pin has since chaperoned me on all my travels.

The most helpful people in the world facilitated my tour of the island. When I hitchhiked, people drove out of their way to deliver me right to the door. Finding a destination was aided by detailed written instructions to be presented to passers-by. I was frequently given a variety of delicious food and treated to lunch. When looking for the bus terminal, I would be escorted, handed a ticket and put on the bus. On being asked for directions to the train station, a man flagged down the nearest car and gave orders to deliver me promptly. I experienced a two-week continuous hospitality shift. Not once was a thank you expected or demanded, but always given.

Thus, the beauty in Taiwan was not to be found in the dreary towns, but in the people themselves; and the wisdom learned, As One Wishes, often takes a turn I least expect.

November 1991

FOKUANGSHAN MONASTERY
Nuns walk the halls with calm purpose.

MADAGASCAR

Madagascar is often described as the eighth continent, so different from Africa are its culture, geography, flora and fauna. It boasts a multitude of ecosystems and an unusually high biodiversity. The Malagasy also have an interesting heritage, a unique mélange of Indonesian, Arab and African stock. The tradition of rice cultivation comes with their Indonesian genes, requiring the practice of "slash and burn," which is rapidly and systematically destroying the natural forests. National parks have been established to stem this destruction. They comprise an extraordinary number of habitat types: lush rain forest, bamboo forests, spiny forest, and dry deciduous forest, but also include coral reefs, desert, sandstone mountains and eroded spires of limestone.

Endemic to the island are lemurs, interesting creatures whose ancestors floated from Africa on rafts of vegetation. In the absence of predators these primates have proliferated into a diverse range of nearly fifty species of all shapes, sizes and habits, from the nocturnal pygmy mouse lemur no bigger than its namesake to the indri of medium bear size. The latter has the loudest call in nature, announcing territorial boundaries — so loud in fact that I had to hold my hands to my ears.

Walking in Kirindy, the national park of dry deciduous forest, I saw many lemurs including a female Verreaux's sifaka and her baby. She was actively foraging in a tree, intent on eating and paying me no heed at all, but the infant noticed me immediately. Shy yet curious, it took a furtive peek and then would bury its head in its mother's fur, repeating the behavior several times. These babies are superbly hard-wired for balance. From the moment after birth when they climb onto their mother's back to when they finally leave it, they never fall.

October 2004

KIRINDY NATIONAL PARK
A juvenile Verreaux's sifaka.

LAOS

The long wooden boat flexed and twisted beneath me as it raced through narrow passages and ran turbulent water on the River Ou. The vessel was somewhat unstable due to the collective imbalance of myself, two oil drums, and a rooster, all perched on the arched bamboo roof. When the river was calm I enjoyed the grand scenery of limestone pinnacles and caves, and watched people cultivating exposed sandbars and panning for gold. Switching to trucks to reach the remote north, I noticed that the road deteriorated as the landscape became more astounding. Limestone cliffs plunged to deep river valleys with thickly forested slopes while the trucks lumbered down thrilling drops on the boulder-strewn tracks.

Reminders of the Vietnam War were ubiquitous. Metal debris was cleverly put to uses entirely different than originally intended: bomb casings used as bridge supports or airplane parts incorporated into huts. Children played inventively with a parachute. In places, the land was scarred with enormous craters from carpet-bombing; although they were most certainly scarred themselves, Laotians showed me touching kindnesses, such as paying for a ferry crossing or pulling out fresher bread from the bottom of the basket.

Tam Phiu is an extensive cave, a shelter for villagers during the war who slept in the day and worked the fields at night. The Americans bombed the hideout and eleven families were killed. Exploring by candlelight I found only rubble, but the cavern dripped with memories and melancholy. Sitting at the entrance as dusk descended I contemplated the folly of war and, spreading out my sarong, I settled to sleep. As I drifted off, a chill breeze blew out of the cave and sent shivers through my body.

February 1995

MUANG NGOI
Transport on the River Ou.

HONG KONG

The tram scaled Victoria Peak at a giddy angle. The seats faced upward, as in a reversed position their contents would tumble out. Tourists pressed downwards on the ascent twisted around and gasped at the view below. Locals faced forward, reading a book or dreaming of dim sum. On each ride I became motion-sick, disoriented by the angled window frames making the adjacent tall apartment blocks appear to be falling backward. Visitors and locals alike were finally treated to that fine vista from the viewing platform at the top of the tramline: the Hong Kong cityscape, Victoria Harbour and Kowloon beyond. Well above the tension between snooty Brit and disgruntled Chinese, I gazed with detached loftiness at the urban busyness of a major world financial center.

Hosted by a friend's brother, I discovered his apartment stood slightly below this viewpoint, the lobby door opening to the tram platform. After a day or two he departed on business, leaving me to luxuriate in a space filled with an eclectic mix of comfy sofas, ornately carved doors and the bric-a-brac collected through years of ex-pat life. Floor-to-ceiling windows, fortified against typhoons by large wooden beams, afforded the same outstanding visual treat. Up there with the gods, I witnessed a pair of kites in full aerial combat scrapping over food or perhaps dating. At night, I was privileged to see the full moon rise over this panorama of sparkling lights.

Victoria Peak is blessed with a network of walking trails, which I explored regularly. I enjoyed getting slightly lost in the luxuriant growth high above a major, densely packed city. These paths delighted the walker with a 360-degree view of Hong Kong Island. One such snapshot juxtaposed a traditional Chinese temple stone lion and the Bank of China Tower (built in a bout of corporate rivalry to surpass the nearby HSBC skyscraper). It typified Hong Kong's meld of the traditional and the modern.

December 1991

HONG KONG ISLAND
A stone lion and the Bank of China Tower.

INDIA

Chandigarh is a city in India like no other. Planned in the early 1950s by the Swiss architect Le Corbusier, it comprises sectors of several city blocks separated by broad tree-lined boulevards. Traffic circulates easily, avoiding the chaos and gridlock typical of Indian cities. Also designed by Le Corbusier, the ultramodern government buildings of the Capitol Complex have a timeless appeal and must have seemed very avant-garde when built.

Not far from the Complex, I stooped low through a small arched opening in a nondescript wall to enter a kingdom the like of which I had never seen. Narrow alleys constructed of rock or sculpted concrete abruptly opened to terraces, large waterfalls, balconies, bridges and high walls with abstract sculptures. All were man-made and each had an otherworldly feel. Retaining walls were faced with river stones or shards of porcelain from plumbing fixtures. Stacked terracotta pots or suspended strings of pebbles formed partitions. I found a tangle of roots to be of concrete.

I wandered through a series of courtyards, where near-life-size human and animal statues stood on raised banks. The individuals of each group — bird, monkey, dog, human, buffalo, elephant or strange mythical creature — were similar, but each unique. All were created in a primitive style. The cast of characters included: beings with human faces on abstract bodies, colorful people constructed of plastic bangles, leering water buffalo with porcelain teeth, and a musical band playing a variety of instruments, accompanied by small white celestial creatures.

Its creator was Nek Chand, a government road inspector, who quietly toiled over a period of forty years to create a "Kingdom of Gods and Goddesses," made solely from found objects, building and road waste, and concrete. I spent hours in this hidden gem of a magical rock garden and was charmed and enthralled by these delightful creations.

December 2010

NEK CHAND'S ROCK GARDEN, CHANDIGARH
A musical band and celestial creatures.

CANADA

In the autumn of 1998, my sister Jill and I traveled the breadth of Canada from Vancouver, British Columbia to St. John's, Newfoundland. We searched out places that had touched our childhood lives and those that figured in our parents' lives long before. As a kind of pilgrimage, we sought homes we had lived in, schools we had attended, my father's places of work, and people who might remember us. We found more than we imagined, and experienced warm and friendly welcomes with much reminiscing. The administrator at the hospital where Jill was born was at first cold and unhelpful, until I mentioned how kind everyone had been thus far. With that she melted and within arm's reach pulled Jill's birth documents from 1952. In Moncton, New Brunswick, hospital staff located our mother's nurse training records from 1938-41, including an eerily unfamiliar file photo.

In a black and white photo taken in 1943, our parents stand at the door of the Ascension Church in Montreal, my mother holding a dozen white roses. We arrived at the church full of awe to be in the very spot where they were married. Our wistfulness was rudely broken when the perplexed staff informed us that the church was only completed in 1944. "Annunciation" can easily be confused with "Ascension," it seems. At the actual church our wonder was somehow dampened, but we took delight in recognizing our parents' distinctive signatures in the marriage register.

On most of our adventure we easily took the rough with the smooth, but when we arrived at my birthplace, St. Michael's Hospital in Lethbridge, Alberta, we were just in time to see bulldozers scrape away the last of the debris. Gazing upon the flattened site, I experienced a deep sense of loss as a distant, but real, part of me had irrevocably slipped away. The trip culminated in Newfoundland, taking us back to our roots at my mother's place of birth. Spending time with her surviving sisters and extended family grounded me again with a feeling of belonging.

September 1998

MONTREAL
The door of the Ascension Church.

UNITED STATES

Imagine a small community where:

~ Citizens burst into action with fundraising events when misfortune befalls a community member

~ A shelter operating year-round feeds and houses the homeless

~ Local produce is sold at farmers' markets where people meet to socialize and enjoy live music

~ Scores of women leap into brisk lake waters while competing in a triathlon, to fund mammograms for women who cannot afford them

~ Children plant daffodils on freeway verges

~ Over a hundred nonprofit organizations supported by volunteers provide services for the area, including the much-loved community radio station

~ Christmas street market stalls brim with artisan-crafted goods and the sounds of minstrels and carolers, evoking traditions of a bygone era

~ People know and help their neighbors

~ Hundreds volunteer annually to clean up and restore the local river

~ High school students have the opportunity to study peace, social justice and sustainability during hands-on semesters

~ An extraordinary number of organic farms and whole-food stores provide healthy food choices

~ At-risk girls are mentored and given opportunities to improve their lives and achieve their goals

~ Supermarkets donate a portion of their profits to local charities

~ Church and charity groups host Thanksgiving and Christmas dinners and several weekly lunches for everyone in the community

~ A vibrant arts and music scene fills the calendar year round

~ School children campaign to prevent the closure of the local state park, and win.

These are the twin towns of Grass Valley and Nevada City, and this is where I live.

September 2010

SCOTTS FLAT LAKE, NEVADA CITY, CALIFORNIA
The hectic start of a fundraising triathlon.

THE AUTHOR

Ayacucho is the guinea pig capital of Peru and therefore the world. I was compelled to taste it. In a fine old colonial-style restaurant, I joined the locals on the patio; the other gringos were upstairs. As the menu did not list guinea pig, I asked the manager, who pondered for a second; then his eyes lit up as he raced away to an outbuilding. Minutes later he reappeared with a small pink limp body and slapped it down on the kitchen counter with panache. Guinea pig was available indeed.

It arrived deep-fried with French fries and salad. It was completely flattened, but the head was still attached, teeth protruding. There was very little meat and I could only find three legs. It tasted like chicken, but had a more delicate, tender flavor. Later, talking to a Peruvian about guinea pigs, I explained that in my country we kept them as pets and we never ate them. "What?" he said, astonished. "Not even the big ones?"

September 2001

ACKNOWLEDGEMENTS

I would like to thank the following people for their advice and help in making this book: Nik Colyer for general publishing advice, Jeff Kane for information on writing proposals, LeeAnn Brook for advice on publishing books, Heather Llewellyn for help with photographs, Michael Llewellyn for the author photo on the back cover, Shera Banbury for proofreading, Kit Bailey whose meticulous editing transformed my manuscript into something readable, and Kathy Dotson for her miracle with the design and layout. Thanks to my sisters Michele and Jill and all my family and friends for their encouragement and enthusiasm for the project. Belated thanks to my father whose artistic talents spawned my photographer's eye, and to my mother whose adventurous spirit gave me an innate desire to see the world.

CPSIA information can be obtained
at www.ICGtesting.com
Printed in the USA
LVIC06n2306061015
457118LV00006BA/21

* 9 7 8 0 9 8 6 1 4 5 1 0 0 *